To

_____

From

_____

Message

_____

_____

_____

From the Heart

© 1995 Christian Art Gifts, RSA
        Christian Art Gifts Inc., IL, USA

First edition 1995
Second edition 2002
Third edition 2003

Designed by Christian Art Gifts

Originally published under the title *From the Heart* by Fleming H. Revell, a division of Baker Book House Company, Grand Rapids, Michigan, 49516, U.S.A. Copyright © 1992 by Virginia J. Ruehlmann and The Helen Steiner Rice Foundation.

Material in this book is adapted from *From the Heart* calendar with permission from Flemming H. Revell.

ISBN 1-86920-137-X

Printed in China

  06 07 08 09 10 11 12 13 14 – 16 15 14 13 12 11 10 9

FROM
THE
HEART

One Minute Devotions

Helen Steiner Rice

christian
art gifts

JANUARY

JANUARY 1

THE NEW YEAR

What will you do
with this year that's so new?
The choice is yours –
God leaves that to you!

*You crown the year
with your bounty.*
Psalm 65:11

Today accept the challenges
and the possibilities of
the year that lies ahead.

JANUARY 2

LIGHT A CANDLE

You can't light a candle
to show others the way
without feeling the warmth
of that bright, little ray.

Light is shed upon the righteous
and joy on the upright in heart.
Psalm 97:11

Today remind yourself
of the radiance and
illumination that can be spread
by just one small flame.

JANUARY 3

ANSWERED PRAYERS

Games can't be won
unless they are played,
and prayers can't be answered
unless they are prayed.

*The LORD detests the sacrifice
of the wicked, but the prayer
of the upright pleases him.*
Proverbs 15:8

Today pray with a
sincere heart. Pray
earnestly and constantly.

JANUARY 4

TENDER HEARTS

We love the sound of laughter
and the merriment of cheer,
but our hearts would lose their tenderness
if we never shed a tear.

*Those who sow in tears will
reap with songs of joy.*
Psalm 126:5

Today appreciate
the importance of both
laughter and tears.

JANUARY 5

GOD FORGIVES

We are all God's children,
and He loves us – every one,
and completely forgives
all that we have done.

Train a child in the way he should go,
and when he is old he will not turn from it.
Proverbs 22:6

Today repeat, "God loves
me and God forgives me."

JANUARY 6

FAITH TO BELIEVE

Trouble is only a challenge
to spur you on to achieve
the best that God has to offer
if you have the faith to believe!

The fear of the LORD is
the beginning of knowledge.
Proverbs 1:7

Today, with faith in your
heart, you can face any trouble
that you encounter.

JANUARY 7

TWO SIDES

There are always two sides –
the good and the bad,
the dark and the light,
the sad and the glad.

*He who seeks good finds
goodwill, but evil comes to
him who searches for it.*
Proverbs 11:27

Today keep an open
mind in all matters.

JANUARY 8

MAKING THE BEST

Stop wishing for things
you complain you have not,
and start making the best
of all that you've got.

*I pour out my complaint before
him; before him I tell my trouble.*
Psalm 142:2

Today be happy with what
you have – not discontent
with what you don't have.

JANUARY 9

JOY AND PEACE

Show us that in quietness
we can feel Your presence near,
filling us with joy and peace
throughout the coming year.

In the shelter of your presence
you hide them from the intrigues
of men; in your dwelling you keep
them safe from accusing tongues.
Psalm 31:20

Today ask Jesus to share your
concerns and confidences.

JANUARY 10

SHOW ME THE WAY

Show me the way,
not to fortune or fame,
not to win laurels
or praise for my name ...
But show me the way
to spread the great story
that Thine is the kingdom,
the power, and the glory.

*I have seen you in the sanctuary and
beheld your power and your glory.*
Psalm 63:2

Today concentrate on ways
to spread the Good News.

JANUARY 11

HIS LOVE

No day is too dark
and no burden too great
that God in His love
cannot penetrate.

Do not be wise in your own eyes;
fear the LORD and shun evil.
Proverbs 3:7

Today whatever occurs, whatever
burden you shoulder, keep
steadfast in your trust of God.

JANUARY 12

HIS LOVING CARE

May He who hears our every prayer
keep you in His loving care –
and may you feel His presence near
each day throughout the coming year.

*The LORD is close to the
brokenhearted and saves those
who are crushed in spirit.*
Psalm 34:18

Today and every day feel
God's presence as you look
for Him in others.

JANUARY 13

LOVE ONE ANOTHER

Love one another
and help those in need,
regardless of color,
race, church, or creed.

*Hatred stirs up dissension, but
love covers over all wrongs.*
Proverbs 10:12

Today concentrate on helping others
and grasp each opportunity to
offer encouragement and assistance.

JANUARY 14

MY BURDEN

Lord, don't let me falter,
don't let me lose my way,
don't let me cease to carry
my burden day by day.

*He says, "I removed the burden
from their shoulders; their hands were
set free from the basket. In your
distress you called and I rescued you."*
Psalm 81:6-7

Today, with God's help, carry
your burdens and seek solutions.

JANUARY 15

A BRAND-NEW START

It does not take a new year
to make a brand-new start,
it only takes the deep desire
to try with all your heart.

*Remove the dross from the
silver, and out comes material
for the silversmith.*
Proverbs 25:4

Today continue to try. Focus
on asking God for help in your
decisions and not relying only
on your own strength.

JANUARY 16

GOD'S UNCHANGING LOVE

In this changing world,
may God's unchanging love
surround and bless you daily
in abundance from above.

*But I pray to you, O LORD, in the time
of your favor; in your great love, O God,
answer me with your sure salvation.*
Psalm 69:13

Today you may not understand
why you are facing adversity or
you may question God's plan, but
someday you will understand it all.

JANUARY 17

A PRAYER FOR HOPE

If you meet God in the morning
And ask for guidance when you pray,
You will never in your lifetime
Face another hopeless day.

Sing to the LORD, you saints
of his; praise his holy name.
For his anger lasts only a moment,
but his favor lasts a lifetime.
Psalm 30:4-5

Today meet and greet the
Lord with hope in your heart.

JANUARY 18

WORSHIP

I come not to ask, to plead,
or implore You,
I just come to tell You
how much I adore You!

*I trust in God's unfailing
love for ever and ever.*
Psalm 52:8

Today express your love for God
in a way that is pleasing to Him ...
by living His commandments.

JANUARY 19

TIME TO BE KIND

Happiness
is just a state of mind
within the reach of everyone
who takes the time to be kind.

He who oppresses the poor shows
contempt for their Maker, but whoever
is kind to the needy honors God.
Proverbs 14:31

Today take the time to befriend
a co-worker or a neighbor. Volunteer
to drive an elderly person to a medical
appointment or cook a meal for a new
mother just home from the hospital.

JANUARY 20

GOD'S MIGHTY HAND

God's mighty hand
can be felt every minute,
for there is nothing on earth
that God isn't in it.

*Sing to the L*ORD *a new song, for he has
done marvelous things; his right hand and his
holy arm have worked salvation for him.*

Psalm 98:1

Today thank God for holding you
in the palm of His hand – a hand
that is both gentle and strong.

JANUARY 21

GOD LOVES YOU

God truly loves you
come what may ...
He will lead you and protect you
every step along life's way!

*Lead me, O LORD, in your
righteousness because of my enemies –
make straight your way before me.*
Psalm 5:8

Today, when seeking a solution to
a problem, confidently take the most
difficult step: the very first step.

JANUARY 22

I LOVE YOU BEST

God, help me in my own small way
to somehow do something each day
to show You that I love You best
and that my faith will stand each test.

I believed; therefore I said,
"I am greatly afflicted."
Psalm 116:10

Today accomplish at least one act
of kindness no matter how small
or insignificant it may seem.

JANUARY 23

A PRAYER FOR FORGIVENESS

Forgive the many errors
that I made yesterday
and let me try again, dear God,
to walk closer in Thy way.

*Then I acknowledged my sin to you and
did not cover up my iniquity. I said, "I
will confess my transgressions to the Lord"
– and you forgave the guilt of my sin.*
Psalm 32:5

Today make a sincere effort to
eliminate errors and those occasions
that could be offensive to God.

JANUARY 24

A GOOD DAY

Every day is a good day
to lose yourself in others,
and any time is a good time
to see mankind as brothers.

A generous man will prosper;
he who refreshes others
will himself be refreshed.
Proverbs 11:25

Today accept others as they are.
When you are friends with others,
you are also a friend with Jesus.

JANUARY 25

LOVE TO THE FULLEST

Each day as it comes,
brings a chance to each one
to live to the fullest,
leaving nothing undone
that would brighten the life
or lighten the load
of some weary traveler lost on life's road.

*Praise be to the Lord, to God our
Savior, who daily bears our burdens.*
Psalm 68:19

Today try through your actions
to reflect God's magnificence and
brilliance into someone else's life.

JANUARY 26

START WITH A PRAYER

Don't start your day by supposing
that trouble is just ahead.
It's better to stop supposing
and start with a prayer instead.

But I cry to you for help,
O LORD; in the morning my
prayer comes before you.
Psalm 88:13

Today start and end
your day with prayer.

JANUARY 27

FIGHT THE GOOD FIGHT

Cling to your standards
and fight the good fight.
Take a firm stand
for things that are right.

*Contend, O LORD, with those
who contend with me; fight
against those who fight against me.*
Psalm 35:1

Today keep your
standards beyond reproach.

January 28

Daily Prayers

Brighten your day
and lighten your way,
lessen your cares
with daily prayers.

Taste and see that the
Lord is good; blessed is the
man who takes refuge in him.
Psalm 34:8

Today pray and you'll find your day
brighter and your way lighter.

JANUARY 29

PURPOSE IN MY DAYS

Bless me, heavenly Father,
forgive my erring ways,
grant me strength to serve Thee,
put purpose in my days.

*The LORD is my strength and my
song; he has become my salvation.*
Psalm 118:14

Today serve the Lord by serving
others. Avoid self-preoccupation.
There are many who need the
assistance that only you can offer.

JANUARY 30

QUIETNESS OF MIND

Give us through the coming year
quietness of mind.
Teach us to be patient.
And always to be kind.

I waited patiently for the LORD;
he turned to me and heard my cry.
Psalm 40:1

Today develop more patience and
value the calm that can be yours.

JANUARY 31

LOOK FOR THE BEST

If you desire to be happy
and get rid of the misery of dread,
just give up supposin' the worst things
and look for the best things instead.

Blessed is the man who finds wisdom,
the man who gains understanding.
Proverbs 3:13

Today look for the good in people,
places, and happenings.

FEBRUARY

FEBRUARY 1

A SWEET SMILE

When you walk down the street,
life will seem twice as sweet
if you smile at the people
you happen to meet!

The cheerful heart
has a continual feast.
Proverbs 15:15

Today let your wardrobe include
a bright, pleasant expression. A ready
smile makes a fashionable accessory.

FEBRUARY 2

HOPE'S RAINBOW

We know above the dark clouds
that fill a stormy sky
hope's rainbow will come shining through
when the clouds have drifted by.

*The light of the
righteous shines brightly.*
Proverbs 13:9

Today look beyond the
stormy formations and seek
to discover the silver lining.

FEBRUARY 3

GO TO GOD IN PRAYER

We all have cares and problems
we cannot solve alone,
but if we go to God in prayer,
we are never on our own.

A wise man listens to advice.
Proverbs 12:15

Today if you feel lonely,
invite Jesus to join you.

FEBRUARY 4

UNDERSTANDING LOVE

Unless we think we're better
than the Father up above,
let us forgive our sisters and brothers
in understanding love.

*Do not say, "I'll do to him as he
has done to me; I'll pay that
man back for what he did."*
Proverbs 24:29

Today seek to forgive and
forget actual or imagined hurts
that have come your way.

FEBRUARY 5

NEVER TOO BUSY

Never be too busy to stop and recognize
the grief that lies in another's eyes,
too busy to offer to help or share,
too busy to sympathize or care.

*Do not withhold good from
those who deserve it, when
it is in your power to act.*
Proverbs 3:27

Today try to identify the
heart-hurt hidden in the words
that another is speaking.

February 6

New awareness

Thank You, God, for the miracles
we are too blind to see,
give us new awareness
of our many gifts from Thee.

*One man pretends to be rich,
yet has nothing; another pretends
to be poor, yet has great wealth.*
Proverbs 13:7

Today develop an abiding sense
of gratitude – an appreciation
for the gifts of our Father.

FEBRUARY 7

REMINISCE

Stop awhile to reminisce
and to pleasantly review
happy little happenings
and things you used to do.

*I remember the days of long ago; I
meditate on all your works and
consider what your hands have done.*
Psalm 143:5

Today be thankful for
pleasant memories.

FEBRUARY 8

SMALL DEEDS

Seldom do we realize
the importance of small deeds
or to what degree of greatness
unnoticed kindness leads.

He holds victory in store for the upright,
he is a shield to those whose walk is
blameless, for he guards the course of the just
and protects the way of his faithful ones.
Proverbs 2:7-8

Today in some manner, no matter
how seemingly small, make the way
smoother for at least one person.

FEBRUARY 9

THE LIFELINE

Don't ever sever the lifeline
that links you to
the Father in heaven
who cares for you.

The fear of the LORD adds length to life,
but the years of the wicked are cut short.
Proverbs 10:27

Today seek ways to assist God as
He continues to care for you.

FEBRUARY 10

DAILY BLESSINGS

No day is unmeetable
if, on rising, our first thought
is to thank God for the blessings
that His loving care has brought.

*Praise the L*ORD*. Give thanks to the L*ORD*,
for he is good; his love endures forever.*
Psalm 106:1

Today reflect on God's goodness.
Appreciate His magnanimity.

FEBRUARY 11

A GOOD ATTITUDE

The nature of our attitude
toward circumstantial things
determines our acceptance
of the problems that life brings.

But I have stilled and quieted my soul;
like a weaned child with its mother,
like a weaned child is my soul within me.
Psalm 131:2

Today minimize problems
instead of exaggerating them.

FEBRUARY 12

KINDER AND WISER

May we try to do better
and accomplish much more
and be kinder and wiser
than in the day gone before.

*The fear of the L*ORD *is the
beginning of wisdom, and knowledge
of the Holy One is understanding.*
Proverbs 9:10

Today establish a deeper understanding
of situations confronting you. Temper
all responses with wisdom and kindness.

FEBRUARY 13

THE HEART'S OPENED DOOR

Love makes us patient, understanding,
and kind, and we judge with our
heart, not with our mind. For as soon
as love enters the heart's opened door, the faults
we once saw are not there anymore.

*Better a meal of vegetables where there
is love than a fattened calf with hatred.*
Proverbs 15:17

Today ask that love color
your vision. Consequently, all
fault-finding will be eliminated.

FEBRUARY 14

LOVE ONE ANOTHER

"Love one another as I have loved you"
may seem impossible to do –
but if you will try to trust and believe,
great are the joys that you will receive.

The wise in heart accept commands,
but a chattering fool comes to ruin.
Proverbs 10:8

Today identify the unloved and
the unwanted in your community
and then reach out to them with
a sign of love and concern.

FEBRUARY 15

GOD'S HELP

God's help never fails
and how much we receive
depends on how much
our hearts can believe.

*You prepare a table before
me in the presence of my
enemies. You anoint my head
with oil; my cup overflows.*
Psalm 23:5

Today your heart and
cup can overflow.

FEBRUARY 16

THE GENEROUS HEART

In the generous heart of loving,
faithful friends, God in His charity
and wisdom always sends
a sense of understanding
and the power of perception
and mixes these fine qualities
with kindness and affection.

Let love and faithfulness never leave you.
Proverbs 3:3

Today act with kindness at all times. Express
your appreciation to those who serve
in countless ways: the bus driver, the mailman,
the schoolteacher, the paperboy.

FEBRUARY 17

GOD'S MIRACLES

God's miracles
are all around,
within our sight
and touch and sound.

*Shout with joy to God, all the
earth! Sing the glory of his
name; make his praise glorious!*
Psalm 66:1, 2

Today take time to observe and
appreciate God's amazing miracles.

FEBRUARY 18

A PRAYER FOR PATIENCE

God, teach me to be patient,
teach me to go slow –
teach me how to wait on You
when my way I do not know.

*A quick-tempered man does foolish
things, and a crafty man is hated.*
Proverbs 14:17

Today pursue the quality
of forbearance.

FEBRUARY 19

THE WAY TO HAPPINESS

Happiness is only found
in bringing it to others,
and thinking of all folks we meet
not as strangers, but as brothers.

He who despises his neighbor sins, but
blessed is he who is kind to the needy.
Proverbs 14:21

Today increase your generosity
and eliminate selfishness.

FEBRUARY 20

A BETTER DAY

God in His mercy looks
down on us all,
and though what we've done
is so pitifully small,
He makes us feel welcome
to kneel down and pray
for the chance to do better
as we start a new day.

Have mercy on me, O God, according to
your unfailing love; according to your great
compassion blot out my transgressions.
Psalm 51:1

Today strive to do better than yesterday.

FEBRUARY 21

A PRECIOUS JEWEL

Friendship is a golden chain,
the links are friends so dear,
and like a rare and precious jewel,
it's treasured more each year.

He who covers over an offense
promotes love, but whoever repeats
the matter separates close friends.
Proverbs 17:9

Today write a letter to someone –
a letter of appreciation, greeting, congratulations,
get well wishes, or cheer.

FEBRUARY 22

KEEP ON SMILING

Just keep on smiling
whatever betide you,
secure in the knowledge
God is always beside you.

*The LORD is near to all who call on
him, to all who call on him in truth.*
Psalm 145:18

Today maintain a happy
expression and a cheerful attitude,
knowing that God is with you.

FEBRUARY 23

LIFE'S PURPOSE

Everyone has his own little niche
no matter how tiny or small,
for every life has a purpose
or we wouldn't be here at all.

**The LORD works out
everything for his own ends.**
Proverbs 16:4

Today examine your talents and,
whatever they are, use them
to help someone in some way.

February 24

THE COMFORT OF PRAYER

Be glad for the comfort
you've found in prayer.
Be glad for God's blessings,
His love and His care.

*The blessing of the Lord brings
wealth, and he adds no trouble to it.*
Proverbs 10:22

Today can be a day of gladness.

FEBRUARY 25

LOSSES INTO GAIN

No one sheds a teardrop
or suffers loss in vain,
for God is always there
to turn our losses into gain.

*For you, O LORD, have delivered
my soul from death, my eyes
from tears, my feet from stumbling.*
Psalm 116:8

Today offer thanks to God for
always staying near to you.

FEBRUARY 26

LOVE DIVINE

"Love divine, all loves excelling"
make my humbled heart Your dwelling,
for without Your love divine
total darkness would be mine.

*He who dwells in the shelter of
the Most High will rest in the shadow
of the Almighty. I will say of the
LORD, "He is my refuge and my
fortress, my God, in whom I trust."*
Psalm 91:1, 2

Today thank Jesus for
illuminating your life.

FEBRUARY 27

LOVE AND TRUST

Just follow God unquestioningly
because you love Him so,
for if you trust His judgment
there is nothing you need know.

From heaven you pronounced judgment,
and the land feared and was quiet –
when you, O God, rose up to judge,
to save all the afflicted of the land.
Psalm 76:8, 9

Today face your problems as they arise. Don't
anticipate trouble. The majority of worries
revolve around problems that never occur.

FEBRUARY 28

WAIT ON GOD

If when you ask for something
God seems to hesitate,
never be discouraged –
He is asking you to wait.

May integrity and uprightness
protect me, because my hope is in you.
Psalm 25:21

Today wait if He asks you.

FEBRUARY 29

PRICELESS TREASURES

A cheerful smile, a friendly word,
a sympathetic nod ...
these are all priceless treasures
from the storehouse of our God.

*A man finds joy in giving an apt
reply – and how good is a timely word!*
Proverbs 15:23

Today offer words of
encouragement to a friend, parent,
relative ... and to yourself.

MARCH

MARCH 1

TAKE UP YOUR CROSS

When your cross gets
a little heavy to wear
and a little bit more
than you think you can bear,
remember how He suffered and died
and allowed Himself to be crucified.

They have pierced my hands and my feet.
Psalm 22:16

Today if your cross seems
heavy, reflect on Jesus, His
suffering and crucifixion.

MARCH 2

THE HAPPINESS WE GIVE

We know that life is never measured
by how many years we live,
but by the kindly things we do
and the happiness we give.

A generous man will himself be blessed,
for he shares his food with the poor.
Proverbs 22:9

Today share a kindness –
a telephone call, a ride, a loaf
of home-made bread –
with someone in need.

MARCH 3

GOD STANDS READY

We awaken in the morning,
wondering how we'll meet the day,
not knowing God stands ready
to help us if we pray.

*The integrity of the upright guides
them, but the unfaithful are
destroyed by their duplicity.*
Proverbs 11:3

Today call upon God for
His heavenly guidance.

MARCH 4

GOD'S WISDOM

Trust God's all-wise wisdom
and doubt our Father never,
for in the kingdom of our Lord
there is nothing lost forever.

*He who walks with
the wise grows wise.*
Proverbs 13:20

Today work on eliminating
doubt and increasing trust.

MARCH 5

MEET WITH GOD

To understand God's greatness
and to use His gifts each day
the soul must learn to meet Him
in a meditative way.

How much better to get wisdom than gold,
to choose understanding rather than silver!
Proverbs 16:16

Today make time to
meditate on God's Word.

MARCH 6

A CROWN OF STARS

There can be no crown of stars
without a cross to bear,
and there is no salvation
without faith and love and prayer.

*Blessings crown the
head of the righteous.*
Proverbs 10:6

Today with faith and love and
prayer as your companions, press on
to newer and higher achievements.

MARCH 7

GUIDED BY HIS HAND

There are many things in life
that we cannot understand,
but we must trust God's judgment
and be guided by His hand.

*The way of the LORD
is a refuge for the righteous.*
Proverbs 10:29

Today let the direction of your
life be guided by God's hand.

MARCH 8

SEASONS OF THE SOUL

Spring always comes with new life and birth
followed by summer
to warm the soft earth –
and what a comfort
to know there are reasons
that souls, like nature,
must have their seasons.

He who goes out weeping, carrying
seed to sow, will return with songs
of joy, carrying sheaves with him.
Psalm 126:6

Today compare the seasons of the
year with the seasons of your soul.

MARCH 9

THE GREATEST RICHES

Seek first His kingdom,
and you will possess
the world's greatest riches
which is true happiness.

Your kingdom is an everlasting
kingdom, and your dominion
endures through all generations.
Psalm 145:13

Today when you write your
"must do" list put "seek
God's kingdom" at the top.

MARCH 10

GOD MADE ALL THINGS

Our Father made the heavens,
the mountains and the hills,
the rivers and the oceans,
and the singing whippoorwills.

Let them praise the name of the Lord,
for he commanded and they were created.
He set them in place for ever and ever; he
gave a decree that will never pass away.
Psalm 148:5, 6

Today be thankful for the
beauty, the peace, and the
marvel found in nature.

MARCH 11

FAITH IN THE LORD

No hill is too high,
no mountain too tall,
for with faith in the Lord
you can conquer them all.

*Find rest, O my soul, in God
alone; my hope comes from him.*
Psalm 62:5

Today repeat over and over,
"With God all things are possible."

MARCH 12

GOD KNOWS BEST

Never complain about your cross,
for your cross has been blest.
God made it just for you to wear
and remember, God knows best!

*Trust in the Lord with all your heart
and lean not on your own understanding;
in all your ways acknowledge him,
and he will make your paths straight.*
Proverbs 3:5, 6

Today accept your cross uncomplainingly – for,
after all, it was personally
created for you by the Master Designer.

MARCH 13

LOOK TO THE SUN

Most of the battles
of life are won
by looking beyond the clouds
to the sun.

When I called, you answered me;
you made me bold and stouthearted.
Psalm 138:3

Today look beyond the clouds and
you'll find some rays of sunshine.

March 14

New friends

May we try
in our small way
to make new friends
from day to day.

*A trustworthy envoy
brings healing.*
Proverbs 13:17

Today focus on the priceless
value of friendship.

MARCH 15

As close as a prayer

The love of God surrounds us
like the air we breathe around us –
as near as a heartbeat,
as close as a prayer,
and whenever we need Him,
He'll always be there.

*The LORD is faithful to all his promises
and loving toward all he has made.*
Psalm 145:13

Today each beat of your heart will
remind you that God is with you.

MARCH 16

OPEN YOUR HEART

Just close your eyes
and open your heart
and feel your worries
and cares depart.

But my eyes are fixed on you,
O Sovereign LORD; in you I take
refuge – do not give me over to death.
Psalm 141:8

Today, as thoughts of God enter
your heart, your worries will leave.

MARCH 17

THE RISEN SAVIOR

In the resurrection
that takes place in nature's sod,
let us understand more fully
the risen Savior, Son of God.

Rise up and help us; redeem us
because of your unfailing love.
Psalm 44:26

Today marvel at the lesson taught
by nature on life, death, resurrection ...
and remembrance of Jesus.

MARCH 18

HIS GRACE IS SUFFICIENT

If we try to stand alone,
we are weak and we will fall,
for God is always greatest
when we're helpless, lost, and small.

*Listen, my son, to your
father's instruction.*
Proverbs 1:8

Today ask God to stand
with you. With God at your side
you can face all challenges.

MARCH 19

GOD'S TOUCH

I see the dew glisten
in crystal-like splendor
while God, with a touch
that is gentle and tender,
wraps up the night and softly tucks it away
and hangs out the sun to herald a new day.

*The sun will not harm you
by day, nor the moon by night.*
Psalm 121:6

Today welcome the freshness of
morning and the opportunities that
await you with the start of a new day.

MARCH 20

HAPPINESS

Happiness is something
we create in our mind,
it's not something you search for
and so seldom find.

You will eat the fruit of your labor;
blessings and prosperity will be yours.
Psalm 128:2

Today be a messenger of happiness.

MARCH 21

TELL HIM YOUR TROUBLES

God's presence is ever beside you,
as near as the reach of your hand.
You have but to tell Him your troubles,
there is nothing He won't understand.

*You have made known to me the path of life;
you will fill me with joy in your presence,
with eternal pleasures at your right hand.*
Psalm 16:11

Today converse with God
and also listen to Him.

MARCH 22

SPRINGTIME AWAKENING

The God who sends the winter
and wraps the earth in death
will always send the springtime
with an awakening breath.

For you have delivered me from death
and my feet from stumbling, that I may
walk before God in the light of life.
Psalm 56:13

Today thank God for the
gift of changing seasons of
nature and the gift of new life.

MARCH 23

GOD IS NEAR

God is no stranger
in a faraway place,
He's as close as the wind
that blows across my face.

He makes clouds rise from the ends of the earth; he sends lightning with the rain and brings out the wind from his storehouses.
Psalm 135:7

Today be aware of the
omnipresence of God.

MARCH 24

A PRICELESS GIFT

Friendship is a priceless gift
that can't be bought or sold,
to have an understanding friend
is worth far more than gold.

*Wounds from a friend
can be trusted, but an
enemy multiplies kisses.*
Proverbs 27:6

Today appreciate the
tremendous value of having
an understanding friend.

MARCH 25

GOD IS LIFE

Every growing, living thing
that you can touch or see at spring
is but a message from above
to say that God is life and love.

*The earth is filled with your love,
O Lord; teach me your decrees.*
Psalm 119:64

Today respond to God's communication
and His deep devotion that repeats itself
over and over in the quality of existence observed
in the season of spring.

MARCH 26

A SUDDEN THRILL

All nature heeds the call of spring
as God awakens everything,
and all that seemed so dead and still
experiences a sudden thrill.

He turned the desert into pools
of water and the parched
ground into flowing springs.
Psalm 107:35

Today answer God's call as
you thrill to the awakening
of the slumbering earth.

MARCH 27

SHOWING LOVE

God, help me in my feeble way
to somehow do something each day
to show You that I love You best
and that my faith will stand each test.

*Test me, O LORD, and try me,
examine my heart and my mind;
for your love is ever before me, and
I walk continually in your truth.*
Psalm 26:2, 3

Today let your faith help
you to pass the test.

MARCH 28

A LIGHT FROM ABOVE

No one discovers the fullness
or the greatness of God's love,
unless they have waited in the darkness
with only a light from above.

*Even in darkness light dawns for
the upright, for the gracious and
compassionate and righteous man.*
Psalm 112:4

Today thank God for being your
safety flashlight ... always charged,
always ready to shine, no matter
what the hour or happening.

MARCH 29

RICH REWARD

Great is your gladness
and rich your reward
when you make life's purpose
the choice of the Lord.

*Humility and the fear
of the LORD bring wealth
and honor and life.*
Proverbs 22:4

Today act with humility.

MARCH 30

BRIGHT TOMORROWS

Every burden borne today
and every present sorrow
are but God's happy harbingers
of a joyous, bright tomorrow.

Know also that wisdom is sweet
to your soul; if you find it,
there is a future hope for you,
and your hope will not be cut off.
Proverbs 24:14

Today cherish God's
message of hope.

MARCH 31

WALK IN HIS LIGHT

May He who hears each little prayer
keep you safely in His care
and make the world around you bright
as you walk daily in His light.

Your word is a lamp to my
feet and a light for my path.
Psalm 119:105

Today welcome someone new
into your circle of friends. Let
God's light shine through you.

APRIL

APRIL 1

A FRESH DAY

You are ushering in another day,
untouched and freshly new,
so here I come to ask You, God,
if You'll renew me, too.

Create in me a pure heart,
O God, and renew a
steadfast spirit within me.
Psalm 51:10

Today seek a renewal in
spirit, a renewal that originates
and rests with God.

APRIL 2

WHO BUT GOD?

Who but God
could make the day
and softly put
the night away?

*The day is yours, and
yours also the night; you
established the sun and moon.*
Psalm 74:16

Today give thought and thanks
to our Creator for the light of
day and comfort of night.

April 3

A SMILE

When you do what you do
with a will and a smile,
everything that you do
will seem twice as worthwhile.

*Continue your love to those who know you,
your righteousness to the upright in heart.*
Psalm 36:10

Today concentrate on your attitude
and your expression. If you wear a
smile you're bound to appear happier and
you might just find you are happier.

APRIL 4

WE ARE HIS

We never meet our problems alone,
for God is our Father and we are His own.
There's no circumstance we cannot meet
if we lay our burden at Jesus' feet.

But he lifted the needy
out of their affliction.
Psalm 107:41

Today invite Jesus to share
your problem and assist
you in seeking a solution.

APRIL 5

IMPORTANT WORK

We cannot all be famous
or be listed in "Who's Who,"
but every person, great or small,
has important work to do.

From the fruit of his lips a man is
filled with good things as surely as
the work of his hands rewards him.
Proverbs 12:14

Today remember that the smallest
deed accomplished with love, the
tiniest talent used for God, the most
minute gesture carried out with kindness
are very important acts in God's eyes.

APRIL 6

TRIUMPH OVER TROUBLE

To triumph over trouble
and grow stronger with defeat
is to win the kind of victory
that will make your life complete.

A man's heart reflects the man.
Proverbs 27:19

Today be encouraged with
thoughts of Jesus and His
victory over apparent defeat.

APRIL 7

A PRIVILEGE TO KNOW

There are some folk we meet in passing
and forget them as soon as they go –
there are some we remember with pleasure
and feel honored and privileged to know.

*A man of understanding
delights in wisdom.*
Proverbs 10:23

Today recall some of the
people who have profoundly
influenced your life.

APRIL 8

SPRINGTIME

Springtime is a season
of hope and joy and cheer ...
there's beauty all around us
to see, and touch, and hear.

*The moon marks off
the seasons, and the sun
knows when to go down.*
Psalm 104:19

Today take time to value the
ability to see – or to touch or
to hear or to smell or to taste.

APRIL 9

BE CHEERFUL

Since fear and dread and worry
cannot help in any way,
it's much healthier and happier
to be cheerful every day.

*A hot-tempered man stirs
up dissension, but a patient
man calms a quarrel.*
Proverbs 15:18

Today be cheerful all day.

APRIL 10

LEARN HOW TO PRAY

Remember me, God?
I come every day
just to talk with You, Lord,
and to learn how to pray.

Listen to my cry for help,
my King and my God,
for to you I pray.
Psalm 5:2

Today picture Jesus sitting next
to you. What will you discuss?
What topics will be covered?

APRIL 11

GOD'S GIVING IS GREATER

No matter how big man's dreams are,
God's blessings are infinitely more,
for always God's giving is greater
than what man is asking for.

He will receive blessing
from the LORD and
vindication from God his Savior.
Psalm 24:5

Today be grateful to God for His
amazing and incredible generosity.

APRIL 12

GREATEST JOY

Memories are priceless possessions
that time can never destroy,
for it is in happy remembrance
the heart finds its greatest joy.

*I thought about the former
days, the years of long ago.*
Psalm 77:5

Today engrave everyday experiences
on your heart and mind as precious and too
quickly passing moments in time. Today's
happenings are tomorrow's memories.

APRIL 13

BREAD ALONE

Man cannot live by bread alone
no matter what he may have or own ...
for though he reaches his earthly goal,
he'll waste away with a starving soul.

I spread out my hands
to you; my soul thirsts for
you like a parched land.
Psalm 143:6

Today the hunger and thirst in
your heart will only be satisfied
with a diet of good works.

APRIL 14

EASTER

An empty tomb,
a stone rolled away
speak of the Savior
who rose on Easter Day.

But I trust in you, O LORD; I say,
"You are my God." My times are
in your hands; deliver me from my
enemies and from those who pursue me.
Psalm 31:14, 15

Today keep the resurrection of
our Lord and its powerful impact
uppermost in your thoughts.

APRIL 15

THE EASTER STORY

All across the waking earth
great nature with perfection
retells the Easter story
of death and resurrection.

*When you send your Spirit,
they are created, and you
renew the face of the earth.*
Psalm 104:30

Today refresh your mind,
body, and spirit. Look around
you. God is rejuvenating the earth.
He can do the same for you.

APRIL 16

A TIME OF JOY

Let not your heart be troubled –
let not your soul be sad –
Easter is a time of joy
when all hearts should be glad.

*We will shout for joy when
you are victorious and will lift up
our banners in the name of our God.*
Psalm 20:5

Today when you see a butterfly
let it remind you of new life.

APRIL 17

LIFE IS ETERNAL

Life is eternal and love is immortal
and death is a gateway, an entrance and portal
into a life that no man can envision,
for God has a greater perspective and vision.

Even though I walk through the
valley of the shadow of death, I will
fear no evil, for you are with me; your
rod and your staff, they comfort me.
Psalm 23:4

Today resolve to improve the manner in which
you live this life in preparation for the next ... for
life is forever, thanks to Jesus.

APRIL 18

SUNSHINE AND RAINBOWS

After the clouds, the sunshine,
after the winter, the spring,
after the shower, the rainbow –
for life is a changeable thing.

The LORD is my light and my
salvation – whom shall I fear?
Psalm 27:1

Today search for the rainbows
that are present in life.

APRIL 19

RENEWAL

After the winter comes the spring
to show us again that in everything
there's always renewal divinely planned,
flawlessly perfect, the work of God's hand.

*For the L*ORD *is the great God, the*
great King above all gods. In his hand
are the depths of the earth, and
the mountain peaks belong to him.
Psalm 95:3, 4

Today renew yourself. Improve yourself. Awaken
the desire within you to blossom
into the best you can be. Let it be accomplished
in and for God's honor.

APRIL 20

THE GLORY AND THE GRACE

Let us see the beauty
and the glory and the grace
that surrounds us in the springtime
as the smiling of God's face.

My soul thirsts for God, for
the living God. When can
I go and meet with God?
Psalm 42:2

Today, if you really look, you
can see God's presence and
presents all around you.

APRIL 21

THE LOVE OF GOD

Kings and kingdoms all pass away,
nothing on earth endures,
but the love of God who sent His Son
is forever and ever yours.

*But you, O LORD, sit enthroned
forever; your renown endures
through all generations.*
Psalm 102:12

Today exalt in the knowledge
that God's love endures forever.

April 22

THE STREET OF DREAMS

Just as we fall beside the road,
discouraged with life,
bowed down with the load,
we lift our eyes,
and what seemed a dead end
is the street of dreams,
where we meet a friend.

The Lord sustains the humble.
Psalm 147:6

Today and every day a friend is
a gift from God – as is Jesus!

APRIL 23

A MUCH BRIGHTER DAY

In sickness or health, in suffering or pain,
in storm-laden skies, in sunshine and rain,
God always is there to lighten your way
and lead you through darkness
to a much brighter day.

He covers the sky with clouds;
he supplies the earth with rain and
makes grass grow on the hills.
Psalm 147:8

Today, whatever the weather or circumstances,
know that darkness will end, dawn will break,
and the sun will rise.

APRIL 24

THE HEAVENLY KING

He who was born to be crucified
arose from the grave to be glorified ...
and the birds in the trees
and the flowers of spring
all join in proclaiming this heavenly King.

*I will praise you, O Lord my
God, with all my heart; I will
glorify your name forever.*
Psalm 86:12

Today add some harmony to the
song that the world is singing.

APRIL 25

WORRY NO MORE

Have you ever heard rumors
you would like to refute
or some telltale gossip
you would like to dispute?
Well, don't be upset for God knows the
score and with God as your judge,
you need worry no more.

A gossip betrays a confidence;
so avoid a man who talks too much.
Proverbs 20:19

Today be Christlike in your spoken
words ... and those left unspoken.

APRIL 26

GOOD RICHES

Good health, good humor,
and good sense,
no man is poor
with this defense.

Pleasant words are a honeycomb, sweet
to the soul and healing to the bones.
Proverbs 16:24

Today share the recipe for a
good life. The main ingredients
include faith in and devotion to God
and service for others.

APRIL 27

A STRONGHOLD FOR THE SOUL

God's love is like an anchor
when the angry billows roll –
a mooring in the storms of life,
a stronghold for the soul.

*The LORD is my rock, my fortress and
my deliverer; my God is my rock, in
whom I take refuge. He is my shield and
the horn of my salvation, my stronghold.*
Psalm 18:2

Today stay firmly and securely
anchored to the Lord.

APRIL 28

GOD IS YOUR FRIEND

God forgives you until the end,
He is your faithful, loyal friend.
Somebody cares and loves you still,
and God is the Someone who always will.

Praise the LORD, O my soul, and forget not all his benefits – who forgives all your sins and heals all your diseases ... who satisfies your desires with good things so that your youth is renewed like the eagle's.
Psalm 103:2-3, 5

Today grasp the significance of having
a faithful, loyal friend. Now be one.

APRIL 29

SHOWERS OF BLESSING

Each day there are showers of blessings
sent from the Father above,
for God is a great, lavish giver
and there is no end to His love.

*You are the God who performs
miracles; you display your
power among the peoples.*
Psalm 77:14

Today count your blessings.

APRIL 30

SPRING BEAUTY

Apple blossoms bursting wide
now beautify the tree
and make a springtime picture
that is beautiful to see.

*O LORD my God, you are very
great ... the earth is satisfied
by the fruit of his work.*
Psalm 104:1, 13

Today enumerate the various hues and
color gradations in the springtime scenes
that you observe and marvel at the
originality and creativity in God's works.

MAY

MAY 1

WHEN YOU SMILE

You'll find when you smile
your day will be brighter,
and all of your burdens
will seem so much lighter.

*I sought the LORD, and he answered
me; he delivered me from all my fears.
Those who look to him are radiant; their faces
are never covered with shame.*
Psalm 34:4, 5

Today will prove that a radiant
smile adds radiance to the day.

MAY 2

JOY FROM THE LORD

You can't do a kindness
without a reward,
not in silver nor gold
but in joy from the Lord.

*May your love and your
truth always protect me.*
Psalm 40:11

Today extend kindness to
someone and unbounded
gladness will return to you.

May 3

A MOTHER'S LOVE

When we think of our mothers,
we draw nearer to God above,
for only God in His greatness
could fashion a mother's love.

My son, keep your father's
commands and do not
forsake your mother's teaching.
Proverbs 6:20

Today pay tribute to your mother.
Her love touched your life and will
continue to influence you forever.

MAY 4

ENJOY THE SUNSHINE

We wouldn't enjoy the sunshine
if we never had the rain.
We wouldn't appreciate good health
if we never had a pain.

*I know, O LORD, that your
laws are righteous, and in
faithfulness you have afflicted me.*
Psalm 119:75

Today study the contrasts in life:
light and darkness, sunshine and rain,
joy and sorrow, good health and pain.
The appreciation deepens when opposite
ends of the spectrum are experienced.

MAY 5

A FRIEND INDEED

We know not how it happened
that in an hour of need
somebody out of nowhere
proved to be a friend indeed!

*Do not forsake your friend
and the friend of your father.*
Proverbs 27:10

Today step into someone's life
and prove your friendship.

MAY 6

TO CARE

To live without caring
is to die from within ...
man loses his drive
and his purpose to win.

*Evil men do not understand
justice, but those who seek
the LORD understand it fully.*
Proverbs 28:5

Today increase your
degree of caring.

MAY 7

A PART TO PLAY

There is no one, no matter how lowly,
who hasn't a part to play,
some little thing to contribute,
something to do or to say.

Better to be a nobody and yet
have a servant than pretend to
be somebody and have no food.
Proverbs 12:9

Today plead for the Lord's
guidance to show you what He has
in mind for you to accomplish.

MAY 8

BEAUTY ALL AROUND

Thank You, God, for the beauty
around me everywhere,
the gentle rain and glistening dew,
the sunshine and the air.

*The eyes of the LORD are
everywhere, keeping watch on
the wicked and the good.*
Proverbs 15:3

Today appreciate the beauty
surrounding you and you'll
recognize that God is here,
there, and everywhere.

MAY 9

CONSTANT REMINDERS

The sky and the stars, the waves and the sea,
the dew on the grass, the leaves on a tree
are constant reminders of God and His nearness,
proclaiming His presence with crystal-like clearness.

Praise him, sun and moon,
praise him, all you shining stars.
Psalm 148:3

Today the marvels of God's creations will
amaze and astound you. Share with a
child the thrill of a glorious sunrise, a dazzling
sunset, or a spectacular starry sky.

MAY 10

YOUR DEAREST WISH

Put your dearest wish
in God's hands today
and discuss it with Him
as you faithfully pray,
and you can be sure
your wish will come true
if God feels that your wish
will be good for you.

May your hand be ready to help me,
for I have chosen your precepts.
Psalm 119:173

Today place your wish in God's hands
and also accept His time schedule.

MAY 11

SUNSHINE AND RAIN

Our Father knows what's best for us,
so why should we complain –
we always want the sunshine
but He knows there must be rain.

*A greedy man stirs up dissension, but
he who trusts in the LORD will prosper.*
Proverbs 28:25

Today trust in God's wisdom
and in His designs. Recognize that
some patterns, as do some days,
require more discipline than others.

MAY 12

A BEAUTIFUL SMILE

Nothing on earth
can make life more worthwhile
than the sunshine and warmth
of a beautiful smile.

*A wicked man puts up a
bold front, but an upright man
gives thought to his ways.*
Proverbs 21:29

Today soften your heart
and your facial expression.

MAY 13

A LOVING MOTHER

God knew, in His great wisdom,
that He couldn't be everywhere,
so He put His little children
in a loving mother's care.

*May your father and mother
be glad; may she who
gave you birth rejoice!*
Proverbs 23:25

Today speak softly and
lovingly. Recall the tender and
kind actions of a loving mother.

MAY 14

MY QUIET PLACE

My garden beautifies my yard
and adds fragrance to the air ...
but it is also my cathedral
and my quiet place of prayer.

*Worship the LORD in
the splendor of his holiness; tremble
before him, all the earth.*
Psalm 96:9

Today, just as a flower's
purpose is to bloom, let your
purpose be to serve.

MAY 15

TREASURED MEMORIES

Memories grow more meaningful
with every passing year,
more precious and more beautiful,
more treasured and more dear.

I remembered my songs
in the night. My heart
mused and my spirit inquired.
Psalm 77:6

Today recall happy happenings
of bygone years and don't
even think of the tearful times.

MAY 16

GOD'S GLORY

Little do we realize
that the glory and the power
of He who made the universe
lies hidden in a flower.

*The heavens declare the
glory of God; the skies proclaim
the work of his hands.*
Psalm 19:1

Today, when you look at
a flower, see God's love
and a message from Him.

MAY 17

THE FLOWER OF FRIENDSHIP

Life is like a garden
and friendship like a flower
that blooms and grows in beauty
with the sunshine and the shower.

*Splendor and majesty are
before him; strength and
glory are in his sanctuary.*
Psalm 96:6

Today plant the seed of friendship
within your heart. With warmth
of love and showers of kindness,
watch friendship flourish.

MAY 18

A NEWBORN SPRING

Let your prayer continue
through a joyous, waking spring
in thanking God for everything
a newborn spring can bring.

When a king's face brightens,
it means life; his favor is
like a rain cloud in spring.
Proverbs 16:15

Today take a lesson from the
season. Spring into action. Replenish
your faith and refresh your soul.

MAY 19

PEACE IN PRAYER

Kneel in prayer in His presence,
and you'll find no need to speak.
For softly in silent communion,
God grants you the peace that you seek.

My soul finds rest in God alone;
my salvation comes from him.
Psalm 62:1

Today go out of your
way to restore harmony.

MAY 20

THE MYSTERY OF CREATION

In the tiny petal of a tiny flower
that grew from a tiny pod,
is the miracle and the mystery
of all creation and God!

*As for man, his days are like grass, he
flourishes like a flower of the field; the
wind blows over it and it is gone,
and its place remembers it no more.*
Psalm 103:15-16

Today contemplate the life, death,
and resurrection visible in nature.

May 21

The hand of God

In everything,
both great and small,
we see the hand
of God in all.

Arise, Lord! Lift up
your hand, O God. Do
not forget the helpless.
Psalm 10:12

Today look for
the handprints of
God everywhere.

MAY 22

UNTOLD STRENGTH

Help us all to realize
there is untold strength and power
when we seek the Lord and find Him
in our meditation hour.

*May all who seek you
rejoice and be glad in you.*
Psalm 70:4

Today ask God to make known
His plan for you ... listen attentively.
He may just whisper it to you.

MAY 23

A TRUE DISCIPLE

He who makes a sacrifice,
so another may succeed,
is indeed a true disciple
of our blessed Savior's creed.

*Gather to me my consecrated
ones, who made a covenant
with me by sacrifice.*
Psalm 50:5

Today contribute to making
someone a better person.

MAY 24

FAITH AND COURAGE

Grant me faith and courage,
put purpose in my days,
show me how to serve Thee
in the most effective ways.

Wait for the LORD;
be strong and take heart
and wait for the LORD.
Psalm 27:14

Today give yourself to the Lord
and offer Him the use of your
hands, your heart, and your mind.

MAY 25

A WONDERFUL THING

God's love endureth forever –
what a wonderful thing to know
when the tides of life run against you
and your spirit is downcast and low.

For great is his love toward us,
and the faithfulness of the LORD
endures forever. Praise the LORD.
Psalm 117:2

Today let God's steadfast
love assist you in improving
your outlook on life.

MAY 26

GOD'S MERCY

God in His great mercy
reaches out to everyone
and forgives the errors
and the shabby things that are done.

*Have mercy on us, O LORD,
have mercy on us, for we have
endured much contempt.*
Psalm 123:3

Today overlook and forget the hurts
and injustices done to you.
Look for and try to understand the
problem within the one who hurt you.

MAY 27

PATIENCE

Give us patience when things disturb,
so we can somehow gently curb
hasty words in anger spoken,
leaving hearts sad and broken.

*A patient man has great
understanding, but a
quick-tempered man displays folly.*
Proverbs 14:29

Today be gentle in your speech,
your thoughts, and your actions.

MAY 28

THE KEY TO HEAVEN

Faith is the key to heaven,
and only God's children hold
the key that opens the gateway
to that beautiful city of gold.

*This is the gate of the
LORD through which
the righteous may enter.*
Psalm 118:20

Today, instead of giving a
sermon for someone to hear, be
a living one for someone to see.

MAY 29

GOD'S WHISPERS

Each time you pick a daffodil
or gather violets on some hill
or touch a leaf or see a tree,
it's all God whispering, "This is Me."

Look to the LORD and his strength;
seek his face always. Remember
the wonders he has done, his miracles,
and the judgments he pronounced.
Psalm 105:4, 5

Today enjoy God's handiwork,
His fingerprints, and loving
touches which abound in nature.

MAY 30

A THANKFUL RESPONSE

The beauty of twilight, the freshness of dawn,
the coolness of dew on a green velvet lawn –
Great is our loss when we no longer find
a thankful response to things of this kind.

He will make your righteousness
shine like the dawn, the justice of
your cause like the noonday sun.
Psalm 37:6

Today respond with deep
appreciation to scenes painted
by our Master Artist.

MAY 31

DEAREST DREAMS

As you climb life's ladder,
take faith along with you,
and great will be your happiness
as your dearest dreams come true.

Love the LORD, all his saints!
The LORD preserves the faithful,
but the proud he pays back in full.
Psalm 31:23

Today let your success be seasoned with
knowledge, perseverance, good judgment,
contentment, optimism, and reliance
on and love of God. When you taste such
success, you're sure to enjoy the flavor.

JUNE

JUNE 1

HIGH IDEALS

You can chart your course in life
with high ideals and love,
for high ideals are like the stars
that light the sky above.

For with you is the fountain
of life; in your light we see light.
Psalm 36:9

Today reflect Christ's
life. Press on!

JUNE 2

SONG OF LOVE

Where there is love,
there is a song
to help when things
are going wrong.

He sang to the LORD the words of this song
when the LORD delivered him from the hand of
all his enemies and from the hand of Saul. He
said: I love you, O LORD, my strength.
Psalm 18:1

Today sing aloud the
melody in your heart.

JUNE 3

THE GIFT OF FRIENDS

When you ask God for a gift,
be thankful if He sends
not diamonds, pearls, or riches,
but the love of real true friends.

A good name is more desirable
than great riches; to be esteemed
is better than silver or gold.
Proverbs 22:1

Today create a positive
experience for those with
whom you come into contact.

June 4

Kindness

What does it matter
if man reaches his goal –
and gains the whole world but loses his soul,
for what have we won if in gaining this end
we've been much too busy
to be kind to a friend?

A kind man benefits himself, but a
cruel man brings trouble on himself.
Proverbs 11:17

Today the most inspiring thing you
can do is to inspire another person.

JUNE 5

THE SUN SHINES THROUGH

We can't have all bright days,
but one thing is true,
no cloud is so dark
that the sun can't shine through!

The man of integrity
walks securely.
Proverbs 10:9

Today make an effort to
enjoy whatever you must do.

JUNE 6

A LITTLE SUNSHINE

To live a little better,
always be forgiving.
Add a little sunshine
to the world in which we're living.

If your enemy is hungry, give
him food to eat; if he is
thirsty, give him water to drink.
Proverbs 25:21

Today add some personal
sunshine to the world around
you – the kind of sunshine that
comes from forgiveness.

June 7

COMFORT

Through the depths of sorrow
comes understanding love,
and peace and truth and comfort
are sent from God above.

*The path of life leads
upward for the wise.*
Proverbs 15:24

Today ask the Lord to help you to
your feet when you fall down.

JUNE 8

A PLACE IN MY HEART

There is happiness in knowing
that my heart will always be
a place where I can hold You
and keep You near to me.

*Honor the L*ORD *with*
your wealth, with the
firstfruits of all your crops.
Proverbs 3:9

Today belong to Jesus – totally,
completely, and absolutely – doing
that which He wants you to do.

JUNE 9

THE JOYOUS GIFT

Thank You, God, for the joyous gift
of feeling the soul's soft, whispering voice
that speaks to me from deep within
and makes my heart rejoice.

Hope deferred makes the heart sick,
but a longing fulfilled is a tree of life.
Proverbs 13:12

Today carefully pay attention
in order to hear that still,
soft, but power-filled voice.

JUNE 10

INNER PEACE

Teach me to let go, dear God,
and pray undisturbed until
my heart is filled with inner peace
and I learn to know Your will!

All a man's ways seem right to him,
but the LORD weighs the heart.
Proverbs 21:2

Today pray to know
and accept God's will.

June 11

SUCCESS

Success is a mixture of good, hard work,
good humor, good luck, and good sense,
and the little tasks of each day, well done,
will bring their own recompense.

*Surely you will reward each person
according to what he has done.*
Psalm 62:12

Today call to mind that old admonition,
"The only place success comes
before work is in the dictionary."

June 12

A SAFE HAVEN

The soul of a man is restless
and just keeps longing for
a haven that is safe and sure
that will last forevermore.

Hear my cry, O God; listen to my
prayer. From the ends of the earth I call
to you, I call as my heart grows faint.
Psalm 61:1, 2

Today remember that you cannot change reality
but you can control the manner
in which you look at things. Your
attitude is under your own control.

JUNE 13

SUMMER BRIGHTNESS

Put the summer brightness in our closed,
unseeing eyes, so in the careworn faces
that we pass, we'll recognize
the heartbreak and the loneliness,
the trouble and despair
that a word of understanding
would make easier to bear.

May your unfailing love be my comfort,
according to your promise to your servant.
Psalm 119:76

Today emphasize being a good listener.
Really listen, hear, and comprehend
what the other person is saying.

185

JUNE 14

A PAUSE TO PRAY

Often during a busy day,
pause for a minute and silently pray.
Mention the names of those you love
and treasured friends you're fondest of.

*The Lord has heard my cry for
mercy; the Lord accepts my prayer.*
Psalm 6:9

Today devote a portion of your
prayers to expressing sincere gratefulness
to God for the privilege of enjoying
friendships – with Him and with others.

JUNE 15

MIRACLES OF LIFE

Miracles are all around,
within our sight and touch and sound,
proclaiming to all doubting men
that in God all things live again.

Who can proclaim the mighty acts of
the LORD or fully declare his praise?
Psalm 106:2

Today, no matter where you
look, know that God is near.

JUNE 16

WISDOM

May I ever be aware
in everything I do
that knowledge comes from learning –
and wisdom comes from You.

*For the LORD gives wisdom,
and from his mouth come
knowledge and understanding.*
Proverbs 2:6

Today make the most of small
opportunities and tasks. They could
just be the start of great things.

JUNE 17

SWEETNESS OF LOVE

Love can't be bought,
it is priceless and free –
love, like pure magic,
is a sweet mystery.

Above all else, guard your heart,
for it is the wellspring of life.
Proverbs 4:23

Today remind yourself
that love comes from above
because God is love.

JUNE 18

ROSES OF KINDNESS

Like roses in a garden,
kindness fills the air
with a certain bit of sweetness
as it touches everywhere.

The tongue that brings healing is a tree of life,
but a deceitful tongue crushes the spirit.
Proverbs 15:4

Today soften some hard hearts with
your kindness. Which do you
prefer – a harsh wind or a mild breeze;
a severe blow or a gentle touch?
Kindness is always the desired choice.

JUNE 19

THE FLOWER OF FRIENDSHIP

Life is a garden,
good friends are the flowers,
and times spent together
life's happiest hours.

Trust in him at all times,
O people; pour out your hearts
to him, for God is our refuge.
Psalm 62:8

Today stroll down memory
lane. Relive and rekindle
treasured friendships.

June 20

Rebounding joy

In making others happy
we will be happy, too,
for the happiness you give away
returns to shine on you.

Make your face shine upon your
servant and teach me your decrees.
Psalm 119:135

Today create happiness.
Happiness is created, never
just found by chance.

JUNE 21

SWEET REST

God's love is like a harbor
where our souls can find sweet rest
from the struggle and the tension
of life's fast and futile quest!

*Be at rest once more, O my soul,
for the LORD has been good to you.*
Psalm 116:7

Today ask the Lord to be
your port of call, His love your
destination and your harbor.

JUNE 22

A BRIDE'S BLESSING

God of love look down and bless
the radiant bride with happiness,
and fill her heart with love's sweet song,
enough to last her whole life long.

Delight yourself in the
LORD and he will give you
the desires of your heart.
Psalm 37:4

Today pray that true love
lives forever. Keep love alive
in your heart and life.

JUNE 23

GOD'S NEARNESS

God comes closest to us
when our souls are in repose ...
like petals dropping soundlessly
from a full-blown rose.

*The LORD is my shepherd, I shall
not be in want. He makes me lie down
in green pastures, he leads me beside
quiet waters, he restores my soul.*
Psalm 23:1-3

Today make your life a
living sanctuary for Jesus.

JUNE 24

FORGIVING LOVE

God asks that we do our best
but He accepts us when we fail,
for no matter what we do to Him
His love and truth prevail.

*Do not withhold your mercy
from me, O LORD; may your love
and your truth always protect me.*
Psalm 40:11

Today look to the future and
become increasingly aware of God
as a forgiving God. The past is past.
He forgives us and loves us.

JUNE 25

WONDERFUL FATHERS

Fathers are just wonderful
in a million different ways,
and they merit loving compliments
and accolades of praise.

***Parents are the pride
of their children.***
Proverbs 17:6

Today cherish your own father and
esteem all fathers. Fathers are educators,
models, providers, and sources of love
for their children. Daily they uphold
the role of hero in their children's eyes.

JUNE 26

WALK WITH GOD

Father, I am well aware
I can't make it on my own,
so take my hand and hold it tight,
for I cannot walk alone.

Though I walk in the midst of trouble,
you preserve my life; you stretch out
your hand against the anger of my foes,
with your right hand you save me.
Psalm 138:7

Today when you walk,
walk with Jesus at your side.

JUNE 27

A GARDEN OF THE HEART

In the garden of the heart
friendship's flower opens wide
when we shower it with kindness
as our love shines from inside.

*You hear, O LORD, the desire
of the afflicted; you encourage
them, and you listen to their cry.*
Psalm 10:17

Today plant the seed of friendship
within your heart. With showers
of kindness and warmth of
love your friendships will grow.

JUNE 28

WALK IN LOVE

Blest are they
who walk in love,
they also walk
with God above.

*For your love is ever
before me, and I walk
continually in your truth.*
Psalm 26:3

Today maintain a loving attitude.

JUNE 29

HILLS OF PEACE

Another hill and sometimes a mountain,
but just when you reach the peak –
your weariness is lifted
and you find the peace you seek.

Turn from evil and do good;
seek peace and pursue it.
Psalm 34:14

Today pray for peace –
within you, your neighbor,
your community, your world.

June 30

Love and peace

May the love of God surround you,
may His peace be all around you,
and may your day be blest
with everything that's happiest.

I love the house where you live, O Lord,
the place where your glory dwells.
Psalm 26:8

Today get to know God better.
Everyone is made in the image of God.
The more you reach out to know people,
the more you learn of God.

JULY

JULY 1

THE LIGHTNESS OF LOVE

Where there is love
the heart is light,
where there is love
the day is bright.

*Let the morning bring me word
of your unfailing love, for I have put
my trust in you. Show me the way I
should go, for to you I lift up my soul.*
Psalm 143:8

Today there will be no
heaviness of heart and no darkness
prevailing because love abounds.

July 2

God's open hands

When trouble surrounds you
and no one understands,
try placing your cares
in God's open hands.

*Into your hands I
commit my spirit.*
Psalm 31:5

Today concentrate on being
optimistic, not pessimistic.

JULY 3

QUIET MEDITATION

When everything is quiet
and we're lost in meditation,
our soul is then preparing
for a deeper dedication.

Oh, how I love your law!
I meditate on it all day long.
Psalm 119:97

Today close out the noise
of everyday living and listen
to that hushed voice deep
within. Meditate in silence.

JULY 4

FREEDOM!

Let the stars and stripes forever
remain a symbol of
a free and mighty nation
built on faith and truth and love!

Righteousness exalts a nation,
but sin is a disgrace to any people.
Proverbs 14:34

Today pray for inspiration
and guidance for the leaders
of our city, state, nation.

July 5

Help for our souls

There's a lot of comfort in the thought
that sorrow, grief, and woe
are sent into our lives sometimes
to help our souls to grow.

He who fears the Lord has
a secure fortress, and for
his children it will be a refuge.
Proverbs 14:26

Today accept your personal disappointments
uncomplainingly. Showers are needed for flowers
to grow and some tears are necessary in our lives
to promote our inner growth.

JULY 6

JOY OF HEART

Thank You, God, for brushing
the dark clouds from my mind
and leaving only sunshine
and joy of heart behind.

*Each heart knows its
own bitterness, and no
one else can share its joy.*
Proverbs 14:10

Today display an unselfish heart.

July 7

God's guidance

Teach me, dear God,
to not rush ahead,
but to pray for Your guidance
and to trust You instead.

*A man's wisdom gives
him patience; it is to his
glory to overlook an offense.*
Proverbs 19:11

Today do not worry. Worry is
like riding a carousel: you keep
going around, but you get nowhere.

JULY 8

THE WINGS OF PRAYER

On the wings of prayer
our burdens take flight –
our load of care
becomes bearably light.

*Cast your cares on the L*ORD
and he will sustain you; he
will never let the righteous fall.
Psalm 55:22

Today with prayer the
rough and trying times
can be made bearable.

JULY 9

THE MERCY OF GOD

Our Father up in heaven
is very much aware
of our failures and shortcomings,
and the burdens that we bear.

My flesh and my heart may
fail, but God is the strength of
my heart and my portion forever.
Psalm 73:26

Today implore God to mend
your broken heart, to tie it back
together with His loving hands.

JULY 10

A BEND IN THE ROAD

Often we stand at life's crossroads
and view what we think is the end,
but God has a much bigger vision
and He tells us it's only a bend.

Show me your ways,
O LORD, teach me your paths.
Psalm 25:4

Today avoid any sign of self-pity.

July 11

A PRAYER OF STRENGTH

Never dread tomorrow
or what the future brings,
just pray for strength and courage
and trust God in all things.

In all your ways acknowledge him,
and he will make your paths straight.
Proverbs 3:6

Today acknowledge your limitations
and your reliance upon God,
remembering that He will supply the
necessary strength to try and try again.
With each day you can begin anew.

July 12

Love's riches

The more you love, the more you'll find
that life is good and friends are kind,
and only what we give away
enriches us from day to day.

What a man desires is unfailing love.
Proverbs 19:22

Today maintain a spirit
of cooperation, harmony,
fidelity and allegiance.

JULY 13

A PRAYER FOR COURAGE

May I never give way to self-pity and sorrow,
may I always be sure of a better tomorrow,
may I stand undaunted come what may,
secure in the knowledge I have only to pray.

*The LORD is gracious and righteous;
our God is full of compassion. The
LORD protects the simplehearted; when
I was in great need, he saved me.*
Psalm 116:5-6

Today do not quit – carry on. Look
ahead, not back. Regret is futile.

JULY 14

RICH BLESSINGS

May He who sends the raindrops
and makes the sunshine, too,
look down and bless you richly
and be very near to you!

*It was you who set all the
boundaries of the earth; you
made both summer and winter.*
Psalm 74:17

Today let the only person you
try to impress be God.

JULY 15

DAILY GRACES

Make us more aware, dear God,
of little daily graces
that come to us with sweet surprise
from never-dreamed-of places.

In you I trust, O my God.
Psalm 25:2

Today ask yourself, "What
lesson can be learned from
the experience of this day?"

JULY 16

LITTLE PRAYERS

Little prayers for little things
fly heavenward on little wings,
and no prayer is too great or small
to ask of God who hears them all.

*Keep me as the apple of
your eye; hide me in the
shadow of your wings.*
Psalm 17:8

Today, this very morning, kneel
to meet and greet the Lord. No
one is ever greater in stature than
when kneeling in prayer to God.

JULY 17

DIVERSITY OF LIFE

Life is a mixture of
sunshine and rain,
teardrops and laughter,
pleasure and pain.

Even in laughter the heart may
ache, and joy may end in grief.
Proverbs 14:13

Today accept disappointments
as well as joys ... even a
beautiful rose has a few thorns.

JULY 18

TALK TO GOD

True communication
is reached through God alone,
to Him the thoughts we cannot express
are understood and known.

*How precious to me are
your thoughts, O God!
How vast is the sum of them!*
Psalm 139:17

Today be faithful in the small
things and you can't help
but be faithful in the large.

JULY 19

HEAR MY PRAYER

Let me serve You every day
and feel You near me when I pray ...
hear my prayer, dear God above,
and make me worthy of Your love!

*Be exalted, O God, above
the heavens; let your glory
be over all the earth.*
Psalm 57:5

Today help to clothe God's
sheep and feed His lambs.

July 20

GOD LOVES US ALL

It's amazing and incredible,
but it's as true as it can be,
God loves and understands us all,
and that means you and me!

My son, do not despise the LORD's
discipline and do not resent his rebuke,
because the LORD disciplines those he
loves, as a father the son he delights in.
Proverbs 3:11-12

Today respect everyone – even those
who appear different from you, for
we are all created by the same Father.

JULY 21

DROPS OF DEW

Into our lives come many things to break
the dull routine, things we had not
planned or that happen unforeseen ...
An unsought word of kindness,
a compliment or two sets the eyes
to gleaming – like crystal drops of dew.

*Like cold water to a weary soul
is good news from a distant land.*
Proverbs 25:25

Today open the window of your
heart and let your light and love shine through.
The happiness you share
with others will circulate back to you.

JULY 22

THY PRESENCE NEAR

In this wavering world of unbelief
we are filled with doubt
and questioning fear –
oh, give us faith in things unseen
so we may feel Thy presence near.

Your path led through the sea, your
way through the mighty waters,
though your footprints were not seen.
Psalm 77:19

Today work on spiritual awareness.

JULY 23

TIME TO BE KIND

In this troubled world it's refreshing to find
someone who still takes the time to be kind.
Someone who's ready
by thought, word, or deed
to reach out a hand in the hour of need.

He who is kind to the poor
lends to the LORD, and he will
reward him for what he has done.
Proverbs 19:17

Today give time to the sick,
needy, and homeless, for if you
ignore them, you ignore God.

227

JULY 24

PRACTICE KINDNESS

If you practice kindness
in all you say and do,
the Lord will wrap His kindness
around your heart and you.

*He who pursues righteousness and
love finds life, prosperity and honor.*
Proverbs 21:21

Today be a source of encouragement.

JULY 25

GOD'S LOVE PROTECTS US

God's love is like a fortress
and we seek protection there
when the waves of tribulation
seem to drown us in despair!

*Then they cried out to the LORD in
their trouble, and he brought them out of their
distress. He stilled the storm to a whisper; the
waves of the sea were hushed.*
Psalm 107:28-29

Today remember that with
only one stroke, a minus (-)
can be turned into a plus (+).

JULY 26

BLESS OUR NATION

God bless our nation
and keep us safe and free,
safe from all our enemies
wherever they may be.

Blessed is the nation whose
God is the LORD, the people
he chose for his inheritance.
Psalm 33:12

Today pray for solutions to national
and international problems.

JULY 27

FAITH IN GOD

Faith makes it wholly possible
to quietly endure
the violent world around us –
for in God we are secure.

*Therefore my heart is glad
and my tongue rejoices; my
body also will rest secure.*
Psalm 16:9

Today trust in God with
deepened conviction. Ask
Him to stay close to you.

July 28

Little gifts

Every happy happening
and every lucky break
are little gifts from God above
that are ours to freely take.

Sing to the Lord, praise his name;
proclaim his salvation day after day.
Psalm 96:2

Today repeat often, "I am someone
special, a unique individual created
by God and filled with potential."

JULY 29

TRUST FOR TODAY

Deal only with the present,
never step into tomorrow,
for God asks us just to trust Him
and to never borrow sorrow.

*In him our hearts rejoice,
for we trust in his holy name.*
Psalm 33:21

Today be flexible,
adaptable, and receptive.

233

JULY 30

A BETTER WORLD

A better world for all mankind
where we are safe and free
must start not with our fellowmen
but within the heart of "me."

*From heaven the LORD looks
down and sees all mankind.*
Psalm 33:13

Today live by the rule that
"peace in the world begins
with me and within me."

JULY 31

BE GLAD

Be glad that you've walked
with courage each day,
be glad you've had strength
for each step of the way.

Direct my footsteps according to
your word; let no sin rule over me.
Psalm 119:133

Today let each step you
take bring you closer to
walking as Jesus walked.

AUGUST

AUGUST 1

AN UNEXPECTED MIRACLE

A word of understanding
spoken in an hour of trial
is an unexpected miracle
that makes life more worthwhile.

*My mouth will speak words of
wisdom; the utterance from my
heart will give understanding.*
Psalm 49:3

Today speak words of
compassion. You can help to
soften the sorrow of a friend.

AUGUST 2

THE SUNSHINE OF LOVE

When the door to our heart
is open wide,
the sunshine of love
will come inside.

*Search me, O God, and
know my heart; test me
and know my anxious thoughts.*
Psalm 139:23

Today practice inward
charm. It cultivates love.
Love radiates from within.

AUGUST 3

THOUGHTS OF PEACE

When I just keep quiet
and think only thoughts of peace
and if I abide in stillness,
my restless murmurings cease.

Be still, and know that I am God.
Psalm 46:10

Today accept yourself with
loving-kindness. Be considerate
of yourself. Take time to think
quietly and peacefully and
enjoy the serenity that emerges.

AUGUST 4

IN FAITH

There's no problem too big
and no question too small,
just ask God in faith
and He'll answer them all.

*Commit to the Lord whatever you
do, and your plans will succeed.*
Proverbs 16:3

Today rejoice in the knowledge
that God listens to each and
every prayer, irrespective of
the magnitude of the request.

AUGUST 5

A HAPPY THOUGHT

Thank You, God, for sending
a happy thought my way
to blot out my depression
on a disappointing day.

*An anxious heart weighs a man
down, but a kind word cheers him up.*
Proverbs 12:25

Today you may not see
any sunbeams, but remember,
the sun is still there.

August 6

Little things

Thank You, God, for little things
that often come our way –
the things we take for granted
but don't mention when we pray.

*Better a little with righteousness
than much gain with injustice.*
Proverbs 16:8

Today thank God for
your many blessings.

AUGUST 7

KNOW GOD

So we may know God better
and feel His quiet power,
let us daily keep in silence
a meditation hour.

*May the words of my mouth and the
meditation of my heart be pleasing in your
sight, O LORD, my Rock and my Redeemer.*
Psalm 19:14

Today enrich your life. Take time to
become better acquainted with God.

AUGUST 8

THE PEACE OF GOD

Peace begins within our own being
where God resides beyond our seeing,
and peace is one thing you'll never find
when you are at war
in your own heart and mind.

For the sake of my brothers and friends,
I will say, "Peace be within you."
Psalm 122:8

Today peace will be with you when
you invite God to dwell within.

AUGUST 9

GROW IN GRATITUDE

Oh, God, who made the summer
and warmed the earth with beauty,
warm our hearts with gratitude
and devotion to our duty.

Enter his gates with thanksgiving
and his courts with praise; give
thanks to him and praise his name.
Psalm 100:4

Today grow in gratitude.

AUGUST 10

MORE LAUGHTER

The more you give,
the more you get –
the more you laugh,
the less you fret!

But the meek will inherit the
land and enjoy great peace.
Psalm 37:11

Today laugh at your mistakes.

AUGUST 11

LOVE'S MANY WAYS

Make us conscious that Your love comes
in many ways; not always just as
happiness or bright and shining days.
Often You send trouble and we foolishly reject it
not realizing that it is Your
will and we should joyously accept it.

*He who spares the rod hates his son, but he
who loves him is careful to discipline him.*
Proverbs 13:24

Today keep in mind that, even during difficult
times, God is transmitting His love and sending
needed discipline into your life.

August 12

Help me, Lord

Lord, don't let me stumble,
don't let me fall and quit,
Lord, please help me find my job
and help me shoulder it.

My son, preserve sound judgment and
discernment, do not let them out of your sight
... Then you will go on your way in safety,
and your foot will not stumble.
Proverbs 3:21, 23

Today practice perseverance.

AUGUST 13

THE WINGS OF PRAYER

Like a soaring eagle
you too can rise above
the storms of life around you
on the wings of prayer and love.

*Have mercy on me, O God, have mercy
on me, for in you my soul takes refuge.
I will take refuge in the shadow of your wings
until the disaster has passed.*

Psalm 57:1

Today a prayer and an expression
of love can lift a depressed spirit.

AUGUST 14

THY WILL BE DONE

Let us be content to solve
our problems, one by one,
asking nothing of tomorrow,
except "Thy will be done."

Do not boast about tomorrow,
for you do not know what
a day may bring forth.
Proverbs 27:1

Today concentrate on
one problem at a time.

AUGUST 15

HEART GIFTS

It's not the things that can be bought
that are life's richest treasure,
it's just the little heart gifts
that money cannot measure.

*Better a little with the fear of the
Lord than great wealth with turmoil.*
Proverbs 15:16

Today appreciate your treasures:
faith, family and friends are the
most valuable and yet are
unavailable for purchase.

AUGUST 16

A CHEERFUL SONG

I sometimes think that friendliness
is like a cheerful song ...
it makes the good days better,
and it helps when things go wrong.

The LORD is my strength and my shield;
my heart trusts in him, and I am
helped. My heart leaps for joy and
I will give thanks to him in song.
Psalm 28:7

Today a song in the heart will
put a smile on the face and
so will calling on a friend.

AUGUST 17

THE HAVEN OF THE HEART

Help all people everywhere
who must often dwell apart,
You know that they're together
in the haven of the heart!

Glorify the LORD with me;
let us exalt his name together.
Psalm 34:3

Today, even though loved ones
are miles away, remember them with
prayers and fond recollections.

AUGUST 18

A QUIET SHELTER

God's love is like an island
in life's ocean vast and wide –
a peaceful, quiet shelter
from the restless, rising tide!

I would hurry to my place of shelter,
far from the tempest and storm.
Psalm 55:8

Today let God's love and
His everlasting arms offer
security and shelter.

AUGUST 19

GOD LOVES US ALL

God knows no strangers,
He loves us all,
the poor, the rich,
the great, the small!

Rich and poor have this in common:
The LORD is the Maker of them all.
Proverbs 22:2

Today introduce someone to God.
God loves to make new friends.

AUGUST 20

FAITH IN YOUR HEART

Faith is a mover of mountains,
and there's nothing that God cannot do,
so start out today with faith in your heart
and climb till your dream comes true!

*Lord, you have been our dwelling
place throughout all generations. Before
the mountains were born or you brought
forth the earth and the world, from
everlasting to everlasting you are God.*
Psalm 90:1-2

Today avoid making
mountains out of molehills.

AUGUST 21

REASSURANCE

Give us reassurance
when everything goes wrong
so our faith remains unfaltering
and our hope and courage strong.

Be strong and take heart,
all you who hope in the LORD.
Psalm 31:24

Today be a living mirror –
reflect your faith in God.

AUGUST 22

FAITH TO ENDURE

Faith to endure whatever comes
is born of sorrow and trials,
and strengthened by daily discipline
and nurtured by self-denials.

My soul is weary with sorrow;
strengthen me according to your word.
Psalm 119:28

Today learn from
your experiences and
errors of yesterday.

AUGUST 23

A BLESSED HOME

Every home
is specially blessed
when God becomes
a daily guest.

*Every day I will praise you and
extol your name for ever and ever.*
Psalm 145:2

Today and every day put out the
welcome mat for Jesus. Invite Him
to enter each heart and home.

AUGUST 24

A WILL AND A SMILE

Do what you do
with a will and a smile
and whatever you do
will be twice as worthwhile.

I desire to do your will, O my
God; your law is within my heart.
Psalm 40:8

Today keep hope in your life
and a smile on your face.

AUGUST 25

CHEERFUL THOUGHTS

Cheerful thoughts like sunbeams
lighten up the darkest fears
for when the heart is happy
there's just no time for tears.

A happy heart makes the face cheerful,
but heartache crushes the spirit.
Proverbs 15:13

Today fill an emptiness in
someone's life rather than
adding to the loneliness.

AUGUST 26

THE GIFT OF UNDERSTANDING

Among the great and glorious gifts
our heavenly Father sends
is the gift of understanding
that we find in loving friends.

*A friend loves at all times, and
a brother is born for adversity.*
Proverbs 17:17

Today locate Jesus in the people you
meet and in everyday happenings.

AUGUST 27

A LITTLE TALK WITH JESUS

When you're feeling downcast,
seek God in meditation,
for a little talk with Jesus
is unfailing medication.

*I delight in your commands because I love
them ... and I meditate on your decrees.*
Psalm 119:47-48

Today remind yourself that a
cheerful disposition is an
outward sign of an inward state.

AUGUST 28

IN GOD'S HANDS

The way we use adversity
is strictly our own choice,
for in God's hands adversity
can make the heart rejoice.

*I will be glad and rejoice in your
love, for you saw my affliction
and knew the anguish of my soul.*
Psalm 31:7

Today demonstrate dependability, for it
is equally as important as your ability.

AUGUST 29

TIME'S SWIFT FLIGHT

Time cannot be halted
in its swift and endless flight
for age is sure to follow youth
like day comes after night.

*Do not cast me away when I am old; do
not forsake me when my strength is gone.*
Psalm 71:9

Today plan for the future since you
are the architect of your own life.

August 30

An eternal light

Love has all the qualities
of an eternal light
that keeps the garments of the soul
clean and pure and bright.

The unfolding of your words gives light;
it gives understanding to the simple …
Turn to me and have mercy on me, as you
always do to those who love your name.
Psalm 119:130, 132

Today pattern your life
after a candle – radiate light
to those around you.

AUGUST 31

THE TEST OF FAITH

It's easy to say, "In God we trust,"
when life is radiant and fair,
but the test of faith is only found
when there are burdens to bear.

*When I am afraid, I will trust in you. In God,
whose word I praise, in God I trust; I will not
be afraid. What can mortal man do to me?*
Psalm 56:3-4

Today learn to profit from
your losses. It's no big deal
to capitalize on gains ... it is
noteworthy to advance after setbacks.

SEPTEMBER

SEPTEMBER 1

A FRAGRANT ROSE

You can't pluck a rose,
all fragrant with dew,
without some of its fragrance
remaining on you.

All the ways of the LORD are
loving and faithful for those who
keep the demands of his covenant.
Psalm 25:10

Today be gentle and kind,
and soon you'll discover that
kindness and gentleness have
become a part of you.

September 2

Look for Jesus

Within the crowded city
where life is swift and fleet
do you ever look for Jesus
upon the busy street?

*Do not hide your face
from your servant ...*
Psalm 69:17

Today be assured you are not
alone – the Lord is with you.

SEPTEMBER 3

GO TO GOD

Whenever I am troubled
and lost in deep despair,
I bundle all my troubles up
and go to God in prayer.

*He will respond to the
prayer of the destitute; he
will not despise their plea.*
Psalm 102:17

Today ponder the question:
"What does God want
me to do with my life?"

SEPTEMBER 4

THE POWER OF PRAYER

Teach us, dear God,
that the power of prayer
is made stronger
by placing the world in Your care!

When a man's ways are pleasing
to the LORD, he makes even his
enemies live at peace with him.
Proverbs 16:7

Today diminish doubt and
increase your faith.

SEPTEMBER 5

CONSTANT KINDNESS

When someone does a kindness
it always seems to me
that's the way God up in heaven
would like us all to be.

*Teach me your way, O LORD, and I will
walk in your truth; give me an undivided
heart, that I may fear your name.*
Psalm 86:11

Today let your actions speak louder than
your words. Give assistance and encouragement
to teachers, principals, and administrators as a
new school term begins.

SEPTEMBER 6

PRAYER

When life becomes a problem
much too great for you to bear,
instead of trying to escape,
just withdraw in prayer.

*A righteous man may have
many troubles, but the Lord
delivers him from them all.*
Psalm 34:19

Today if you experience a
disappointment, deal
with it; don't let it multiply.

SEPTEMBER 7

SEASONS OF LOVE

Through a happy springtime
and a summer filled with love,
may we walk into the autumn
with our thoughts on God above.

*A cheerful heart is good
medicine, but a crushed
spirit dries up the bones.*
Proverbs 17:22

Today value the beauty of
the changing season. No
matter the time of year there is
evidence that God is near.

SEPTEMBER 8

LOVELY MIRACLES

God sends His little angels
in many forms and guises,
they come as lovely miracles
that God alone devises.

Your hands made me and
formed me; give me understanding
to learn your commands.
Psalm 119:73

Today study the lesson of faith, hope, and love
that comes with the arrival of a "special" child.
Broaden your perspective. Become
a friend to a handicapped individual.

SEPTEMBER 9

THE JOY OF ENJOYING

Take nothing for granted,
for whenever you do,
the joy of enjoying
is lessened for you.

*Like clouds and wind without
rain is a man who boasts
of gifts he does not give.*
Proverbs 25:14

Today the most memorable
happening will be the one in
which you helped someone else.

SEPTEMBER 10

GOD LOVES YOU STILL

Somebody cares and always will,
the world forgets but God loves you still.
You cannot go beyond His love
no matter what you're guilty of.

*You are forgiving and
good, O Lord, abounding in
love to all who call to you.*
Psalm 86:5

Today display compassion and
forgiveness, and remember God
forgives you and loves you.

SEPTEMBER 11

UNCHANGING LOVE

Seasons come and seasons go and with them comes the thought of all the various changes that time in its flight has brought. But one thing never changes, it remains the same forever, God truly loves His children and He will forsake them never.

Do not hide your face from me, do not turn your servant away in anger; you have been my helper. Do not reject me or forsake me, O God my Savior.
Psalm 27:9

Today seek ways to encourage the elderly, the middle-aged, or the young.

SEPTEMBER 12

PEACE OF PRAYER

Prayer is much more
than just asking for things –
it's the peace and contentment
that quietness brings.

*Guide me in your truth and teach
me, for you are God my Savior, and
my hope is in you all day long.*
Psalm 25:5

Today experience the "prayer" that
resides in your heart. Use your silent
solitude to enrich your day and to
elevate the calm that is within you.

SEPTEMBER 13

THIS NEW DAY

What will you do
with this day that's so new?
the choice is yours –
God leaves that to you!

*This is the day the L*ORD *has
made; let us rejoice and be glad in it.*
Psalm 118:24

Today and every day keep
your priorities straight –
keep first things first.

SEPTEMBER 14

GOOD THINGS

Let us see in others
not their little imperfections,
but let us find the good things
that arouse our best affections.

*Starting a quarrel is like
breaching a dam; so drop the
matter before a dispute breaks out.*
Proverbs 17:14

Today develop the ability to
look for and find Jesus in others.

SEPTEMBER 15

ALL DAY WITH GOD

Meet God in the morning
and go with Him through the day
and thank Him for His guidance
each evening when you pray.

*In the morning, O LORD, you hear
my voice; in the morning I lay my requests
before you and wait in expectation.*
Psalm 5:3

Today join with God early in the
morning and stay in His company
all day and through the night.

SEPTEMBER 16

LOVE'S WAYS

Love works in ways
that are wondrous and strange.
There's nothing in life
that love cannot change.

A gentle answer turns away wrath,
but a harsh word stirs up anger.
Proverbs 15:1

Today be an example of
agape love. Be patient, kind,
forgiving, and humble.

SEPTEMBER 17

TRUST GOD

It's hard to believe
that God asks no more
than to bring Him our problems
and then close the door.

*The LORD is a refuge for the
oppressed, a stronghold in times of
trouble. Those who know your name
will trust in you, for you, LORD,
have never forsaken those who seek you.*
Psalm 9:9, 10

Today trust and obey, and
tomorrow obey and trust.

SEPTEMBER 18

A REASON TO REJOICE

In trouble and gladness
we can always hear Your voice,
if we listen in silence
and find a reason to rejoice.

The voice of the Lord is powerful;
the voice of the Lord is majestic.
Psalm 29:4

Today listen for and enjoy
the laughter of children.
God is in their midst.

SEPTEMBER 19

I HAVE SOUGHT MY GOD

I have worshiped in churches and chapels,
I have prayed in the busy street,
I have sought my God and have found Him
where the waves of the ocean beat.

*Come, let us bow down in worship, let
us kneel before the LORD our Maker.*
Psalm 95:6

Today, oceanside, countryside,
or mountainside, in a cottage
or in a chalet, know that God
is present when you pray.

SEPTEMBER 20

HEAR ME WHEN I PRAY

Help me when I falter,
hear me when I pray,
receive me in Thy kingdom
to dwell with Thee someday.

*One thing I ask of the LORD, this is
what I seek: that I may dwell in
the house of the LORD all the days of
my life, to gaze upon the beauty of the
LORD and to seek him in his temple.*
Psalm 27:4

Today, if you stumble, know that
God is willing and ready to assist
you to your feet. Do not fear.

SEPTEMBER 21

A BEACON BURNING BRIGHT

God's love is like a beacon,
burning bright with faith and prayer,
And through the changing scenes of life
we can find a haven there!

*They were glad when it grew calm, and
he guided them to their desired haven.*
Psalm 107:30

Today be an active captain of
your life. Direct your course
toward God's haven. He is your
navigator and your lighthouse.

SEPTEMBER 22

WONDERFUL WORLD

God is so lavish in all that He's done
to make this great world such a wonderful one;
His mountains are high
His oceans are deep, and vast and
unmeasured the prairielands sweep.

In his hand are the depths of the earth,
and the mountain peaks belong to him.
Psalm 95:4

Today admire the artistry of God: purple
mountain peaks, white-capped oceans of blue,
golden-hued fields of wheat. God's palette of
colors remains unmatchable.

SEPTEMBER 23

HOPE FOR EVERYDAY

God, grant me courage
and hope for every day,
faith to guide me along my way,
understanding and wisdom, too,
and grace to accept what life gives me to do.

Listen to advice and accept instruction,
and in the end you will be wise.
Proverbs 19:20

Today maintain your purpose in
life, act on it, don't just wish for
it to happen. Persevere in your
attempts to achieve your goal.

SEPTEMBER 24

A HEART OF KINDNESS

Give me understanding,
enough to make me kind,
So I may judge all people
with my heart and not my mind.

*He will judge your
people in righteousness.*
Psalm 72:2

Today evaluate the critical
remarks that come your way.
Sort, keep what helps, and
throw the rest away.

SEPTEMBER 25

GIVE OUR BEST

The future is not ours to know
and it may never be –
so let us live and give our best
and give it lavishly.

There is surely a future hope for you,
and your hope will not be cut off.
Proverbs 23:18

Today remember that what you think of
yourself is more important than what
others think of you. You must therefore
think, live, and approve of how you live.

September 26

Across the miles

Father, hear this little prayer,
reach across the miles from here to there,
so I can feel much closer to those I'm
fondest of and they may know I think
of them with thankfulness and love.

*Answer me when I call to you, O my righteous
God. Give me relief from my distress; be
merciful to me and hear my prayer.*
Psalm 4:1

Today and tonight capture thoughts of
your absent loved ones. Look through
your scrap-books and photograph
albums. Pray for your loved ones.

SEPTEMBER 27

THE TRIUMPH OF FAITH

Faith is a force that is greater
than knowledge or power or skill,
and the darkest defeat turns to triumph
if we trust in God's wisdom and will.

Trust in the LORD and do good;
dwell in the land and enjoy safe
pasture ... Commit your way to the
LORD; trust in him and he will do this.
Psalm 37:3, 5

Today look at the world with
a vision magnified by the power
of faith deep within you.

SEPTEMBER 28

BRIGHTEN LIVES

Do not sit and idly wish for wider, new dimensions where you can put in practice all your good intentions, but at the spot God placed you, begin at once to do little things to brighten up the lives surrounding you.

*The path of the righteous is like
the first gleam of dawn, shining ever
brighter till the full light of day.*
Proverbs 4:18

Today concentrate on your
God-given talents and use
them to help someone.

SEPTEMBER 29

GOD IS ALWAYS THERE

Dear God, what a comfort
to know that You care
and to know when I seek You,
You will always be there!

*The LORD will keep you from all harm –
he will watch over your life; the LORD
will watch over your coming and
going both now and forevermore.*
Psalm 121:7-8

Today knock and seek and
you'll find God waiting for
you. He will console you,
soothe you, and care for you.

SEPTEMBER 30

GOD IS BESIDE YOU

Always remember
that whatever betide you,
you are never alone
for God is beside you.

God is our refuge and strength,
an ever-present help in trouble.
Psalm 46:1

Today be thankful for
God's companionship.

OCTOBER

OCTOBER 1

GOD UNDERSTANDS

Whenever you are troubled,
put your problems in God's hand,
for He has faced all problems
and He will understand.

Trouble and distress have come upon me,
but your commands are my delight.
Psalm 119:143

Today do not be concerned
about outward appearances; rather
concentrate on the necessity and
importance of inner beauty.

OCTOBER 2

LET GOD TALK TO YOU

When your day is pressure-packed
and your hours are all too few,
just close your eyes and meditate
and let God talk to you.

*May my meditation be pleasing
to him, as I rejoice in the LORD.*
Psalm 104:34

Today, if God delays in
answering your prayer, continue
to keep the faith, knowing that
God has His own timetable.

October 3

STEPPING-STONES

Welcome every stumbling block
and every torn and jagged rock,
for each one is a stepping-stone
to God, who wants you for His own.

*He lifted me out of the slimy pit, out
of the mud and mire; he set my feet on a
rock and gave me a firm place to stand.*
Psalm 40:2

Today view your problems with
a spiritual perspective. See each
difficulty as a lesson in problem-
solving and endurance.

OCTOBER 4

THE GOODNESS OF GOD

Wait with a heart that is patient
for the goodness of God to prevail,
for never do our prayers go unanswered
and His mercy and love never fail.

*Be still before the LORD
and wait patiently for him.*
Psalm 37:7

Today call to Him. Display your
patience and be a peacemaker.

OCTOBER 5

THE JOY THAT YOU GIVE

Time is not measured
by the years that you live,
but by the deeds that you do
and the joy that you give.

*Those who plan what is good
find love and faithfulness.*
Proverbs 14:22

Today recognize the importance of
doing an act of kindness. One
small deed accomplished is better than
a hundred unfulfilled promises.

OCTOBER 6

A PLEA FOR PEACE

"Thou wilt keep him in perfect peace
whose mind is stayed on Thee ..."
and, God, if anyone needs peace
it certainly is me!

A man's spirit sustains him in sickness,
but a crushed spirit who can bear?
Proverbs 18:14

Today avoid being judgmental.
Eliminate resentment and bitterness,
and your personal peace will increase.

OCTOBER 7

THE THOUGHTS OF THE HEART

There's something we should not forget –
that people we've known or heard of
or met by indirection have a big part
in molding the thoughts
of the mind and the heart.

In his heart a man plans his course,
but the LORD determines his steps.
Proverbs 16:9

Today display enthusiasm, confidence,
commitment, and determination.
Your zeal for living and your love
of God could be contagious.

OCTOBER 8

LET HIM LEAD YOU

Take the Savior's loving hand
and do not try to understand,
just let Him lead you where He will,
through pastures green, by waters still.

*Know that the LORD is God. It is he
who made us, and we are his; we
are his people, the sheep of his pasture.*
Psalm 100:3

Today follow the Shepherd.
Encourage the sheep who have
strayed to return to the fold.

OCTOBER 9

A RECIPE FOR LIFE

Take a cup of kindness,
mix it well with love,
add a lot of patience
and faith in God above.

Through patience a ruler can be persuaded,
and a gentle tongue can break a bone.
Proverbs 25:15

Today blend kindness, love,
and patience. Sift in a generous
amount of faith. You'll have a
no-fail recipe for life.

OCTOBER 10

A KIND, LOVING HEART

Some folks grow older
with birthdays, it's true,
but others grow nicer
as years widen their view.
No one will notice a few little wrinkles
when a kind, loving heart
fills the eyes full of twinkles.

Children's children are a crown to the aged.
Proverbs 17:6

Today fill an emptiness in someone's
life. Irrespective of age, you
can add happiness and eliminate
loneliness in another person's day.

OCTOBER 11

WORDS UNSPOKEN

Prayer is so often just words unspoken,
whispered in tears
by a heart that is broken ...
for God is already deeply aware
of the burdens we find too heavy to bear.

*I am feeble and utterly crushed;
I groan in anguish of heart.*
Psalm 38:8

Today exemplify tolerance and
forgiveness. Promote reconciliation
with those who have offended you.

OCTOBER 12

WITH THE HELP OF GOD

Only with the help of God
can we meet the vast unknown ...
even the strongest of us cannot
do the job alone!

*Hasten, O God, to save me; O
LORD, come quickly to help me.*
Psalm 70:1

Today flex your spiritual
muscles. Warm up, tone, and
exercise your values and ideals.

OCTOBER 13

LIVE ABUNDANTLY

The more you do unselfishly,
the more you live abundantly ...
the more of everything you share,
the more you'll always have to spare.

*My heart is not proud, O LORD, my eyes are
not haughty; I do not concern myself with
great matters or things too wonderful for me.*
Psalm 131:1

Today contemplate the
magnitude of tasks that can be
accomplished if there is no concern
with receiving praise or credit.

OCTOBER 14

FAITH AND HOPE AND PRAYER

May the people of all nations
at last become aware
that God will solve
the people's problems
through faith and hope and prayer!

*I am your servant; give me discernment
that I may understand your statutes.*
Psalm 119:125

Today take pride in your country
and in those who defend it.

OCTOBER 15

YOUR SOUL'S RICH REWARD

The love you give to others
is returned to you by the Lord,
and the love of God
is your soul's rich reward.

*One man gives freely, yet gains
even more; another withholds
unduly, but comes to poverty.*
Proverbs 11:24

Today heal wounds.
Healing has a domino effect.

OCTOBER 16

OBEY GOD

Let nothing sway you
or turn you away
from God's old commandments –
they are still new today.

*Praise the L<small>ORD</small>. Blessed is the
man who fears the L<small>ORD</small>, who
finds great delight in his commands.*
Psalm 112:1

Today live by God's standards,
not the world's standards.

OCTOBER 17

REAL CONTENTMENT

It's by completing
what God gives us to do
that we find real contentment
and happiness, too.

Repay them for their deeds and for
their evil work; repay them for what
their hands have done and bring
back upon them what they deserve.
Psalm 28:4

Today eliminate procrastination.
Complete the task before you.

OCTOBER 18

GOD'S NEAR YOU

Instead of just idle supposing
step forward to meet each new day
secure in the knowledge
God's near you
to lead you each step of the way.

*When you walk, your steps
will not be hampered; when you
run, you will not stumble.*
Proverbs 4:12

Today accept the challenge that
rests in the dawning of each new day.
Appreciate God's presence and guidance.
He will protect you if you stumble.

OCTOBER 19

GOD IS ALL AROUND YOU

If you would find the Savior,
no need to search afar –
for God is all around you,
no matter where you are!

You hem me in – behind and before;
you have laid your hand upon me.
Psalm 139:5

Today be alert to God's presence –
in yourself, in others, in nature.

OCTOBER 20

THROUGH THE DAY

I meet God in the morning
and go with Him through the day,
then in the stillness of the night
before sleep comes, I pray.

*I rise before dawn and cry for help; I
have put my hope in your word. My eyes
stay open through the watches of the night,
that I may meditate on your promises.*
Psalm 119:147-148

Today, whatever the hour, wherever
the place, assemble your thoughts
and prayers and with a thankful
heart present them to God.

OCTOBER 21

REST IN GOD

I pray that God will just take over
all the problems I couldn't solve,
and I'm ready for tomorrow
with all my cares dissolved.

But I will sing of your strength,
in the morning I will sing of your
love; for you are my fortress,
my refuge in times of trouble.
Psalm 59:16

Today release your worries into God's
hands. Solutions are His specialty.

OCTOBER 22

THE HOUSE OF PRAYER

The house of prayer is no farther away
than the quiet spot
where you kneel and pray,
for the heart is a temple when God is there
as you place yourself in His loving care.

*I will bow down toward your holy
temple and will praise your name
for your love and your faithfulness.*
Psalm 138:2

Today remember that any place is
a good place to pray and thank God.

OCTOBER 23

THE SPIRIT GROWS SERENE

Growing older only means
the spirit grows serene,
and we behold things with our souls
that our eyes have never seen.

*Even when I am old and gray, do
not forsake me, O God, till I declare
your power to the next generation,
your might to all who are to come.*
Psalm 71:18

Today appreciate those who
are older. Value their advice.
Seek their companionship.

OCTOBER 24

GOLDEN FRIENDSHIP

The golden chain of friendship
is a strong and blessed tie,
binding kindred hearts together
as the years go passing by.

*Do good, O LORD, to those who are
good, to those who are upright in heart.*
Psalm 125:4

Today polish your chain of
friendship. Keep it tarnish-free.

OCTOBER 25

THE MASTER BUILDER

God is the master builder,
His plans are perfect and true,
and when He sends you sorrow,
it's part of His plan for you.

For you, O God, tested us;
you refined us like silver.
Psalm 66:10

Today sculpt and work on your life –
for you are creating a masterpiece –
a work of art in partnership with God.

OCTOBER 26

STRENGTH FOR THE DAY

God did not promise sun without rain;
light without darkness, or joy without pain –
He only promised us strength for the day
when the darkness comes
and we lose our way.

*If I say, "Surely the darkness will hide me and the
light become night around me," even the darkness
will not be dark to you; the night will shine
like the day, for darkness is as light to you.*
Psalm 139:11-12

Today generate understanding
and radiate love. Try turning the light
on in the life of another individual.

OCTOBER 27

THE BLESSINGS OF FRIENDSHIP

Father, make us kind and wise
so we may always recognize
the blessings that are ours to take
and the friendships that are ours to make.

*A man of many companions may
come to ruin, but there is a friend
who sticks closer than a brother.*
Proverbs 18:24

Today restore any broken
relationship. Maintain and
support your friendships.
A friend is a gift from God.

OCTOBER 28

A MOTHER'S LOVE

A mother's love is something
that no one can explain,
it is made of deep devotion
and of sacrifice and pain.

Her children arise and call her blessed;
her husband also, and he praises her.
Proverbs 31:28

Today honor and remember your
mother in an appropriate manner –
a visit, a prayer, a message.

OCTOBER 29

THE BITTER AND THE SWEET

Everything is by comparison,
both the bitter and the sweet,
and it takes a bit of both of them
to make our lives complete.

*He who is full loathes honey, but to the
hungry even what is bitter tastes sweet.*
Proverbs 27:7

Today maintain an attitude of
thanksgiving. Be thankful for all
events in your life: sorrows and
joys, failures and successes, the
valleys and the mountains.

OCTOBER 30

DEEPER BEAUTY

Discipline in daily duty
will shape your life for deeper beauty,
and as you grow in strength and grace,
the more clearly you can see God's face.

May God be gracious to us and bless
us and make his face shine upon us.
Psalm 67:1

Today strict training and self-
control will result in an increase
of mercy and effective power.

OCTOBER 31

THE MASTER PLAN

All things work together
to complete the master plan,
and God up in heaven
can see what's best for man.

*But you, O God, are my king from of
old; you bring salvation upon the earth.*
Psalm 74:12

Today cooperate with God, dedicate
and consecrate your efforts to Him,
and you'll be pleasantly surprised
by the Master of the Universe.

NOVEMBER

NOVEMBER 1

STRONG SPIRITS

Whenever we are troubled
and life has lost its song,
it's God testing us with burdens
just to make our spirit strong!

My comfort in my suffering is this:
Your promise preserves my life.
Psalm 119:50

Today face your challenges with
determination and resiliency.

NOVEMBER 2

HIS GREATNESS

Whatever we ask for
falls short of God's giving,
for His greatness exceeds
every facet of living.

*Great is the LORD and most worthy of
praise; his greatness no one can fathom.*
Psalm 145:3

Today be liberal in your praise
of and your gratitude to God.
The degree of His generosity is
beyond compare and the scope
of His giving is unfathomable.

The fragrance of flowers

We rob our own lives much more than
we know when we fail to respond or in
any way show our thanks for the blessings that
are daily ours – the warmth
of the sun, the fragrance of flowers.

All you have made will praise you, O Lord; your
saints will extol you. They will tell of the glory
of your kingdom and speak of your might,
so that all men may know of your mighty acts
and the glorious splendor of your kingdom.
Psalm 145:10-12

Today cultivate an appreciation
for the beauty in nature.

November 4

A hand outstretched

A warm, ready smile
or a kind, thoughtful deed
or a hand outstretched in an hour of need
can change our outlook
and make the world bright
where a minute before
just nothing seemed right.

An offended brother is more unyielding
than a fortified city, and disputes
are like the barred gates of a citadel.
Proverbs 18:19

Today bring a brilliance to the world around you
with a smile and an act of kindness.

November 5

To be peaceful

To be peaceful, I must be kind
for peace can't exist in a hate-torn mind,
so to have peace I must always show
love to all people I meet, see, or know.

He who scorns instruction will pay for it,
but he who respects a command is rewarded.
Proverbs 13:13

Today erase all signs of hatred –
let love and peace prevail.

NOVEMBER 6

FOLLOW HIM

Teach me to be patient
in everything I do,
content to trust Your wisdom
and to follow after You.

*Do not fret because of evil men or be
envious of the wicked, for the evil
man has no future hope, and the lamp
of the wicked will be snuffed out.*
Proverbs 24:19-20

Today practice patience.
Practice makes perfect.

NOVEMBER 7

RELATION WITH GOD

Take ample time
for heartfelt conversation,
establish with our Father
an unbreakable relation.

A word aptly spoken is like
apples of gold in settings of silver.
Proverbs 25:11

Today converse with God
morning, noon, and night.

NOVEMBER 8

GOD, THE CREATOR

Someday may man realize
that all the earth, the seas, and skies
belong to God who made us all,
the rich, the poor, the great, the small!

My mouth is filled with your praise,
declaring your splendor all day long.
Psalm 71:8

Today feel the awe and the
wonder of God's creation.

November 9

Prayers of praise

Prayers are not meant for obtaining
what we selfishly wish to acquire,
for God in His wisdom refuses
the things that we wrongly desire.

*I remember your ancient laws,
O Lord, and I find comfort in them.*
Psalm 119:52

Today infuse your prayers with
praise and thanksgiving to God.

November 10

GOODNESS AND MERCY

Not money or gifts or material things,
but understanding and the joy that it brings,
can change this old world and
its selfish ways and put goodness
and mercy back into our days.

*By wisdom a house is built, and
through understanding it is established;
through knowledge its rooms are
filled with ... beautiful treasures.*
Proverbs 24:3-4

Today give someone a piece of your time,
wrapped with understanding and compassion.
These are gifts that money can't buy.

November 11

Tender memories

Tender little memories
of some word or deed
give us strength and courage
when we are in need.

Surely he will never be shaken; a
righteous man will be remembered forever.
Psalm 112:6

Today reflect upon a past kindness
and the strength it afforded both
the giver and the receiver.

NOVEMBER 12

GRACE TO ENDURE

The more we endure
with patience and grace,
the stronger we grow
and the more we can face.

*The LORD is the strength of his people, a
fortress of salvation for his anointed one.*
Psalm 28:8

Today grow stronger as you adopt
the policy of patiently addressing
the problems that confront you.

NOVEMBER 13

THE REWARDS OF KINDNESS

Kindness is a virtue
given by the Lord,
it pays dividends in happiness
and joy is its reward.

The wicked man earns deceptive
wages, but he who sows
righteousness reaps a sure reward.
Proverbs 11:18

Today add kindness to
someone else's life and your own
happiness will be multiplied.

NOVEMBER 14

THE FULLNESS OF LIVING

The joy of enjoying
and the fullness of living
are found in the heart
that is filled with thanksgiving.

There is deceit in the hearts of those who plot
evil, but joy for those who promote peace.
Proverbs 12:20

Today let your heart overflow with
gratitude and your joy will increase.

November 15

The wonders of the world

It's a wonderful world and it always will be
if we keep our eyes open and focused to see
the wonderful things man is capable of
when he opens his heart to God and His love.

God looks down from heaven on the
sons of men to see if there are any
who understand, any who seek God.
Psalm 53:2

Today unlock the chambers of your
heart and ask God to enter in.
His presence will transfuse your life.

NOVEMBER 16

GOD'S CREATIVE HAND

In the beauty of a snowflake
falling softly on the land
is the mystery and miracle
of God's great, creative hand!

Praise the LORD from the earth ...
lightning and hail, snow and clouds,
stormy winds that do his bidding.
Psalm 148:7-8

Today observe the loveliness of a
wintry scene. Each snowflake, like
each human being, is special and has
its own individual characteristics.

NOVEMBER 17

GOD HEARS

I'm way down here!
You're way up there!
Are You sure You can hear
my faint, faltering prayer?

Hear my prayer, O LORD, listen
to my cry for help; be not deaf to my
weeping. For I dwell with you as an
alien, a stranger, as all my fathers were.
Psalm 39:12

Today call to God. He hears
you always and at all times.

November 18

A PRAYER FROM THE HEART

I give to You my thanks
and my heart kneels to pray –
God keep me and guide me
and go with me today.

*You guide me with your counsel, and
afterward you will take me into glory.*
Psalm 73:24

Today ask God to guide,
guard, and go with you.

November 19

A prayer of thanks

Help us to remember
that the key to life and living
is to make each prayer a prayer of thanks
and every day "Thanksgiving."

*I will praise God's name in song
and glorify him with thanksgiving.*
Psalm 69:30

Today be thankful for your blessings and share
with those not so well-blessed. Be grateful for
your talents. Use some degree
of those talents to help those in need.

NOVEMBER 20

GOD'S KINDNESS

God's kindness is ever around you,
always ready to freely impart
strength to your faltering spirit,
cheer to your lonely heart.

When anxiety was great within me,
your consolation brought joy to my soul.
Psalm 94:19

Today express your thanks
to Jesus for touching your life.

Joy without measure

God's heavens are dotted with uncounted
jewels, for joy without measure is one
of God's rules. His hand is so generous,
His heart is so great, He comes not
too soon, and He comes not too late.

In the beginning you laid the
foundations of the earth, and the
heavens are the work of your hands.
Psalm 102:25

Today realize that God needs no
alarm clocks, wristwatches, or timers.

NOVEMBER 22

GOODNESS AND MERCY

God, I know that I love You,
and I know without doubt
that Your goodness and mercy
never run out.

*Surely goodness and love will
follow me all the days of my life.*
Psalm 23:6

Today count the many
ways that you observe God's
goodness and mercy.

NOVEMBER 23

THE GREATNESS OF GOD

"The earth is the Lord's
and the fullness thereof" –
it speaks of His greatness,
it sings of His love.

*The heavens are yours, and
yours also the earth; you founded
the world and all that is in it.*
Psalm 89:11

Today reflect on the greatness
of our Creator as you
listen to the earth's melody.

NOVEMBER 24

A WORD OF PRAYER

Do you pause in meditation
upon life's thoroughfare,
and offer up thanksgiving –
or say a word of prayer?

*My tongue will speak of
your righteousness and of
your praises all day long.*
Psalm 35:28

Today devote a portion of your
day to reflecting on God's role in
your life and your role in God's plan.

November 25

Faith to believe

Do justice, love kindness,
walk humbly with God –
with these three things
as your rule and your rod
all things worth having
are yours to achieve
if you follow God's words
and have faith to believe!

*The LORD loves righteousness and justice;
the earth is full of his unfailing love.*
Psalm 33:5

Today apply Christ's principles.

NOVEMBER 26

LIGHT A CANDLE

An unlit candle gives no light,
only when burning,
is it shining bright,
and if life is empty, dull and dark,
it's doing things for others
that gives the needed spark.

*You, O LORD, keep my lamp burning;
my God turns my darkness into light.*
Psalm 18:28

Today light up someone's life and you'll
generate happiness for yourself.

PLACE OF PROTECTION

Remember God loves you
and wants to protect you,
so seek that small haven
and be guided by prayer
to that place of protection
within God's loving care.

*Every word of God is flawless; he is a
shield to those who take refuge in him.*
Proverbs 30:5

Today seek safety and security
in God's everlasting arms.

NOVEMBER 28

A SINCERE HEART

It doesn't matter where we pray
if we honestly mean the words we say,
for God is always listening to hear
the prayers that are made
by a heart that's sincere.

In the day of my trouble I will
call to you, for you will answer me.
Psalm 86:7

Today pray with
sincerity and simplicity.

NOVEMBER 29

WHAT WE NEED

If we put our problems in God's hand,
there is nothing we need understand.
It is enough to just believe
that what we need we will receive.

If I rise on the wings of the dawn,
if I settle on the far side of the sea,
even there your hand will guide me,
your right hand will hold me fast.
Psalm 139:9, 10

Today let go and let God
help solve your dilemma.

God guide me today

All I need do
is to silently pray –
"God, help me and guide me
and go with me today."

*Good and upright is the Lord;
therefore he instructs sinners in his
ways. He guides the humble in what
is right and teaches them his way.*
Psalm 25:8-9

Today keep God as your
constant companion.

DECEMBER

DECEMBER 1

THE GIFT OF PEACE

With our hands we give gifts that money
can buy; diamonds that sparkle like stars
in the sky, but only the heart can give
away the gift of peace and a perfect day.

The LORD gives strength to his people;
the LORD blesses his people with peace.
Psalm 29:11

Today ask yourself, "If I were gift
wrapped as a package for Jesus, would
He be pleased to receive me? Do I concentrate
too much on the outward wrappings
and not enough on what's inside?"

DECEMBER 2

DAILY PRAYER

Whenever you are hurried
and must leave something undone
be sure it's not your prayer to God
at dawn or setting sun.

It is good to praise the LORD and make
music to your name, O Most High,
to proclaim your love in the morning
and your faithfulness at night.
Psalm 92:1-2

Today and every day
make time to pray.

DECEMBER 3

PEACE OF MIND

What must I do to ensure peace of mind?
Is the answer I'm seeking too hard to find?
How can I know what God wants me to be?
How can I tell what's expected of me?

Many are the plans in a man's heart,
but it is the LORD's purpose that prevails.
Proverbs 19:21

Today study yourself. Persevere
in accomplishing that which God
has in mind for you to do.

DECEMBER 4

LOVE DIVINE

What is love? No words can define it.
It's something so great,
only God could design it.
Yes, love is beyond what man can define,
for love is immortal and God's gift is divine.

Give thanks to the Lord of lords ...
to him who alone does great
wonders, His love endures forever.
Psalm 136:3-4

Today surprise someone with a phone call or a
joyous greeting. Permit God's love to overflow
through you and your actions.

DECEMBER 5

SWEET FORBEARANCE

Teach me sweet forbearance
when things do not go right,
so I remain unruffled
when others grow uptight.

If you falter in times of trouble,
how small is your strength!
Proverbs 24:10

Today demonstrate forbearance
in your language, your actions,
and your reactions. A calm,
well thought out response has
a soothing effect on others.

DECEMBER 6

A HEART OF PEACE

Teach me how to quiet
my racing, rising heart,
so I may hear the answer
You are trying to impart.

My son, give me your heart and
let your eyes keep to my ways.
Proverbs 23:26

Today calm someone else's fears and
maintain a serenity of your own.

DECEMBER 7

REFLECTIONS OF GOD'S FACE

The silent stars in timeless skies,
the wonderment in children's eyes,
a rosebud in a slender vase
are all reflections of God's face.

*Hear my voice when I call, O LORD; be merciful
to me and answer me. My heart says of
you, "Seek his face!" Your face, LORD, I will
seek. Do not hide your face from me.*
Psalm 27:7-9

Today observe your surroundings
with a spiritual vision. You'll locate
God in places never before imagined.

DECEMBER 8

A PILGRIMAGE OF PRAYER

Prayers are the stairs that lead to God,
and there's joy every step of the way
when we make our pilgrimage to Him
with love in our hearts each day.

*If the Lord delights in a man's
way, he makes his steps firm.*
Psalm 37:23

Today revive your weary heart with
prayer as you climb closer to God.

DECEMBER 9

PEACE OF SOUL

Only by the grace of God
can we gain self-control,
and only meditative thoughts
can restore our peace of soul.

*I will lie down and sleep in peace, for you
alone, O LORD, make me dwell in safety.*
Psalm 4:8

Today if you have a difference
of opinion with someone, disagree
but don't be disagreeable.

DECEMBER 10

MEMORIES TO TREASURE

Memories to treasure
are made of Christmas Day,
made of family gatherings
and children as they play.

*Your wife will be like a fruitful vine
within your house; your sons will be
like olive shoots around your table.*
Psalm 128:3

Today treasure remembrances of the past
and joys of the present by sharing your
love with family members, children,
grandchildren, relatives, or friends.

DECEMBER 11

THE FIRST CHRISTMAS DAY

May the holy remembrance
of the first Christmas Day
be our reassurance
Christ is not far away.

*From birth I was cast upon you; from my
mother's womb you have been my God.*
Psalm 22:10

Today live your life in such a
manner that others can look for
and recognize Jesus within you.

DECEMBER 12

WARMTH AND WONDER

May every heart and every home
continue through the year
to feel the warmth and wonder
of this season of good cheer.

*When anxiety was great within me, your
consolation brought joy to my soul.*
Psalm 94:19

Today pledge to maintain all
year the warmth of love and cordiality generated
by this Christmas season.

December 13

The promise of glory

Make us aware
that the Christmas story
is everyone's promise
of eternal glory.

*Not to us, O Lord, not to us but
to your name be the glory, because
of your love and faithfulness.*
Psalm 115:1

Today send some of your own
love into the world. You don't
have to buy it, box it, wrap it,
tie it – just give love away.

DECEMBER 14

COUNT YOUR BLESSINGS

In counting our blessings,
we find when we're through
we've no reason at all
to complain or be blue.

A faithful man will be richly blessed.
Proverbs 28:20

Today count your loved ones as your top
priority and blessing. It is also important to be
remembered by your loved ones. For which
reason, characteristic, personality
trait, or act of kindness do you wish to be
remembered? Think about it. Work on it.

DECEMBER 15

MEANINGFUL LIVING

If we lived Christmas each day as we should,
and make it our aim to always do good,
we'd find the lost key to meaningful living
that comes not from getting,
but from unselfish giving.

They are always generous and lend
freely; their children will be blessed.
Psalm 37:26

Today live by the principle,
"It's far more blessed
to give than to receive."

DECEMBER 16

HOPE AND GLADNESS

Just like the seasons that come and go
when the flowers of spring
lay buried in snow,
God sends to the heart
in its winter of sadness
a springtime awakening
of new hope and gladness.

*But now, Lord, what do I
look for? My hope is in you.*
Psalm 39:7

Today clear away the icy feelings
of despair and uncover the
gladness buried in your heart.

DECEMBER 17

THE CHRISTMAS STAR

It matters not who or what your are,
all men can behold the Christmas Star.
For the Star that shone is shining still
in the hearts of men of peace and goodwill.

Create in me a pure heart, O God,
and renew a steadfast spirit within me.
Do not cast me from your presence
or take your Holy Spirit from me.
Psalm 51:10-11

Today trim your life with
an inner beauty. The Star
shines for one and all.

DECEMBER 18

GLAD TIDINGS

In the glad tidings
of the first Christmas night,
God showed us
the way and the truth and the light.

*Send forth your light and your truth, let them
guide me; let them bring me to your holy
mountain, to the place where you dwell.*
Psalm 43:3

Today appreciate the magnificent
and generous gift of God's love.

DECEMBER 19

HE HOLDS THE WORLD

Humbly, I realize that He
who made the sea and skies
and holds the whole world in His hand
also has my small soul in His command.

The law of the LORD is perfect, reviving
the soul ... The commands of the LORD
are radiant, giving light to the eyes.
Psalm 19:7-8

Today acknowledge the vastness and
also the gentleness of God's power.
The depths, breadths, lengths, and
widths of the universe are God's creations
and the control rests in His hands.

DECEMBER 20

NEW HOPE

God, make us aware that in Thy name
the Holy Christ Child humbly came
to live on earth and leave behind
new faith and hope for all mankind.

*I wait for the LORD, my soul waits,
and in his word I put my hope.*
Psalm 130:5

Today radiate with the glow
of Christmastime. Jesus came to
earth as a baby. Look for the
innocence, purity, goodness,
and love in those around you.

DECEMBER 21

GIFTS OF CHRISTMAS

The gifts that we give have no purpose
unless God is part of the giving,
and unless we make Christmas a pattern
to be followed in everyday living.

*A gift opens the way for the giver and
ushers him into the presence of the great.*
Proverbs 18:16

Today share a gift with your
feathered, flying friends. The birds
will appreciate water, suet, and
seed. God made all creatures.

DECEMBER 22

A GIFT FROM ABOVE

Christmas to me
is a gift from above –
a gift of salvation
born of God's love.

Love and faithfulness meet together;
righteousness and peace kiss each other.
Psalm 85:10

Today decorate your life with glad
tidings, cheer, and an inner glow
that develops through loving Jesus
and living in a manner pleasing to Him.

DECEMBER 23

GOD'S PATTERN FOR LIVING

Christmas is more than a day at the end
of the year, more than a season of joy
and good cheer; Christmas is really
God's pattern for living, to be
followed all year by unselfish giving.

I will praise you, O LORD, with all my heart ... for
your love and your faithfulness ... (You) have
exalted above all things your name and your word.
Psalm 138:1-2

Today accept the treasured gift from
God called peace! Peace is found in
your own year-round manner of
living when patterned after Jesus' life.

DECEMBER 24

REAL CONTENTMENT

By completing what God
gives us to do,
we find real contentment
and happiness, too.

Whoever gives heed to instruction prospers,
and blessed is he who trusts in the LORD.
Proverbs 16:20

Today awaken the laughter
in your heart and relax a
little in these hectic days.

DECEMBER 25

CHRISTMAS MIRACLES

Miracles are marvels
that defy all explanation
and Christmas is a miracle,
not just a celebration.

*I will give thanks to the LORD because
of his righteousness and will sing praise
to the name of the LORD Most High.*
Psalm 7:17

Today marvel at the
significance and meaning of
the miracle of Christmas.

DECEMBER 26

GLAD TIDINGS

By keeping Christ in Christmas we are
helping to fulfill the glad tidings of the angels
– "Peace on earth and to men, goodwill."

*I will listen to what God the LORD will
say; he promises peace to his people, his
saints – but let them not return to folly.*
Psalm 85:8

Today respond to someone else's
anger with gentleness on your part.
Anger begets anger so put a halt to the
cycle. Greater strength is shown by
those who choose kindness as a reaction.

DECEMBER 27

A BABY

A baby is a gift of life
born of the wonder of love –
a little bit of eternity,
sent from the Father above.

*Sons are a heritage from the L*ORD*,*
children a reward from him.
Psalm 127:3

Today consider the glory,
the wonder, and the beauty
involved in the gift of life.

DECEMBER 28

A FORTRESS OF FAITH

Be not disheartened by troubles,
for trials are the building blocks
on which to erect a fortress of faith
secure on God's ageless rocks.

*In you, O LORD, I have taken
refuge; let me never be put to shame ...
for you are my rock and my fortress.*
Psalm 71:1, 3

Today when adversities mount view them as
stepping-stones to higher ground. Display
courage and inner fortitude when misfortunes
befall you. Be assured, God is ever near.

DECEMBER 29

QUIETNESS OF MIND

At this holy season
give us quietness of mind,
teach us to be patient
and help us to be kind.

*Let them give thanks to the
LORD for his unfailing love and
his wonderful deeds for men.*
Psalm 107:31

Today eliminate condemnation and
display compassion. Kindness is
appreciated now and anytime of the year.

DECEMBER 30

THE SWEETNESS OF PEACE

After the night, the morning,
bidding all darkness cease,
after life's cares and sorrows,
the comfort and sweetness of peace.

O LORD, the God who saves me,
day and night I cry out before you.
Psalm 88:1

Today practice stability
and dependability. They
are just as necessary in life
as having an ability.

DECEMBER 31

THE VOICE OF GOD

Above the noise and laughter
that is empty, cruel, and loud,
do you listen for the voice of God
in the restless, surging crowd?

*Your love, O LORD, reaches to the
heavens, your faithfulness to the skies.*
Psalm 36:5

Today observe the relationship
of happiness and helpfulness:
the extent of your happiness is
commensurate with the degree
of your helpfulness to others.